THE RABBI

OF

84th

STREET

THE RABBI

OF

84th

STREET

THE EXTRAORDINARY LIFE OF

HASKEL BESSER

WARREN KOZAK

HarperCollins*Publishers*

HarperCollins books may be purchased for educational, business, or sales promotional use. For information, please write: Special Markets Department, HarperCollins Publishers Inc., 10 East 53rd Street, New York, NY 10022.

FIRST EDITION

Designed by Joseph Rutt

Printed on acid-free paper

Library of Congress Cataloging-in-Publication Data

Kozak, Warren.

The rabbi of 84th Street : the extraordinary life of Haskel Besser / Warren Kozak.—1st. ed.

p.   cm.

ISBN 0-06-051101-X

1. Besser, Haskel, 1923– 2. Rabbis—New York (State)—New York—Biography. 3. Hasidim—New York (State)—Biography. 4. Rabbis—Israel—Biography. 5. Manhattan (New York, N.Y.)—Biography. I. Title.

BM755.B553K69   2004

296.8'33'092—dc22

[B]

2003056976

04 05 06 07 08 ❖/RRD 10 9 8 7 6 5 4 3 2

To Ronald S. Lauder, who brought Rabbi Besser into my life and the lives of so many others.

And to Lisa and Claire.

ACKNOWLEDGMENTS

In the spring of 1988, I was hired to write a PBS documentary on the fiftieth anniversary of Kristallnacht. The film was sponsored by Ronald S. Lauder, who was just returning from his posting in Vienna, having served as the U.S. ambassador to Austria. That experience (in the middle of the Waldheim controversy) changed his life forever and, although I couldn't know it at the time, it would have a profound impact on my life as well.

When I first came to the Lauder offices, I was surprised to see an elderly Hasidic rabbi who looked out of place in the corporate suite in midtown Manhattan. Although I was curious, I was reluctant to introduce myself because even though I always felt a strong connection to my religion, I was not Orthodox and thought the rabbi might not be interested in meeting me. I couldn't have been more wrong.

It was Rabbi Besser who first invited me into his office and, with his warmth, his sense of humor, and his open mind, he greeted me as an equal. That was the start of an unusual friendship that would grow as the rabbi invited me into his world. Over the past fifteen years, I've had the amazing good fortune to celebrate Shabbos and holidays at Rabbi and Mrs. Besser's table, I've had the opportunity to get to know the extraordinary Besser family, which, for me, stands out as beacon of hope for the future of the American family, and, most of all, I've had the gift of the rabbi's immense knowledge and his friendship.

It should be obvious that a friendship between a Conservative Jew who forgot most of what he learned in Hebrew school and a brilliant Hasidic rabbi is unusual at the outset. But it says more about Rabbi Besser than it does me. My friends who have met the Rabbi realize immediately what makes him unique. To others who ask me about the relationship and what makes him special, I have a stock answer: Rabbi Besser makes the idea of faith plausible at a time when many people have turned away from G-d. This is no small task in the twenty-first century. Add to that a charm and wit that are equally unusual in this day and age and you begin to understand how lucky I have felt for the good fortune of walking into his office fifteen years ago.

I would be remiss if I did not add a special thank you to Sharon Blum who helped put the project together and joined me one morning a week in the rabbi's study as he unfolded his long and fascinating life for us. After those meetings, Sharon and I would often walk down 84th Street in the cold of winter or the warmth of summer, look at each other and say in unison: "What an amazing story!" My thanks also to Marjorie Federbush for her support, along with Basia Jakubowska, Jacob Schuster, Charles Goldstein, Paulette McDougall, Mark Reiter, and Susan Friedland.

Perhaps the greatest support came from home and my wife, Lisa, who in large and small ways helped the project and me along. I am happy my greatest fear was not realized—I began this project when my wife was nine months pregnant and managed to finish it before our daughter's chupah.

And finally to Ronald S. Lauder, who has enriched my life and the lives of more people than we could ever count with his kindness, his generosity, and his vision.

New York City
September 2003

CONTENTS

PROLOGUE

The doormen at the elegant building on Manhattan's Upper West Side—like most doormen everywhere—know the building's tenants mainly by the schedules they keep. But after fifty years, they still don't quite know what to make of the building's perhaps most unusual resident, Haskel Besser.

On the one hand, the man is rigorously predictable—so much so that the doormen can set their watches by his movements. But there are a number of oddities that still leave them scratching their heads after all this time. First, Haskel Besser never seems to sleep. Most nights, if he's not on a plane to Eastern Europe or the Middle East or Washington on *business,* he comes home by cab between midnight and 2 A.M. Yet he is still out the door every morning at 6:30 sharp, before most of his neighbors are even awake (he's actually been up and working since 4:30).

The other oddity the doormen can count on day or night—and this is really surprising, considering Haskel

Besser's backbreaking schedule—is that this man is always smiling. Not just any smile. It's a smile that follows the laws of nuclear physics in that it sets off a chain reaction. People smile when they see him smiling. With his flowing white beard and a twinkle in his eye, he seems to possess that rare alchemy that simply makes people happy when they see him.

The reason for the nonstop schedule is not that he is a type-A personality. This is hardly a frenetic man—he is actually quite calm. But he seems to have pushed at least three lifetimes into the one he was given because he feels he has an enormous debt to pay. And Haskel Besser is a man who has made it a point throughout his life never to be in debt.

A long time ago in what could only be described as another world, Haskel Besser was given an extraordinary opportunity and—while he is very grateful for it—he has spent much of his life trying to understand why it came to him.

Hasidic Jews believe that every human being on earth has been given the greatest gift possible—the gift of life. What that person makes of it, how he spends it, whether it's in honest hard work and study or idle sloth, is up to the individual. People can work to improve themselves and make the world a better place than when they arrived or they can do nothing, leaving the work for others. It's their choice.

Haskel Besser was taught this as a child. It made a huge impression on him. And because he believes it with all his heart, he has spent his life—now more than eighty years— using his great charm, swift intelligence, and unusual capacity for hard work in the pursuit of three goals:

He has conducted his entire life with the goal of bringing honor to his G-d and his people.

He has single-handedly tried to undo a terrible wrong that happened before most of the people on earth today were even born, despite the fact that he was not responsible for it.

And he has spent his life studying and learning so that he might someday understand why, while all people on earth are given the gift of life, he received that precious inheritance not once, but twice.

THE RABBI

OF

84th

STREET

ONE

CROSSING THE STREET

What Haskel Besser does best—and he does a lot of things very well—is demolish any preconceptions people may have of religious Jews.

On the one hand, he is indeed a Hasidic rabbi with a black suit, a black fedora, and that long gray beard. His appearance is always immaculate and he never deviates from it, no matter what the season. If he's just going down to the corner to buy a newspaper, he wears a suit with a vest, starched white shirt with cuff links, and a tie.

Partly that's because of the European tradition in which he was raised. But this immaculate attention to image also gives away another detail of his personality. He understands his context in the greater, non-Jewish world, and he knows that when he walks out his door, people will judge not Haskel Besser, but all rabbis and, hence, all Jews, by the way he conducts himself. That's never far from his mind and accounts, in part, for his courtly manners that are both charming and somewhat out of place in twenty-first-century

America. This is a gentleman in the old sense of the word. It is also someone who takes his position very seriously.

Besides the suit and tie, there is one more crucial piece of attire: he always has a yarmulke on his head—outside, inside, anywhere. (And on Shabbos and Jewish holidays, he wears a streimel—a round, fur hat Hasidic men don on special occasions.)

Many years ago, when Haskel Besser was a young man living in British Palestine, a prospective *colleh* (bride) asked him why he continued to wear this outfit, which may have made sense in Poland, but seemed to make no sense in the airless humidity and heat of Tel Aviv.

"She had a point," the rabbi admits. "It *was* uncomfortable. But I dressed that way then and now because my father and his father did the same."

Traditions, for Rabbi Besser, come in all sorts of large and small packages and he considers all of them important. But there is another crucial facet to this man's personality that sets him apart from many other equally observant Jews who dress the same way and follow the customs of their forefathers. He is also very much a part of the outside, non-Jewish world. His circle of friends includes Jews and non-Jews. He has a deeply sophisticated knowledge of literature, music, and politics. And while his understanding of Talmud and Torah is legendary and he is respected by the most famous rebbes in the world, his admirers extend far beyond that world. He has been an invited guest at White House dinners and presidential inaugurations. He is the recipient of one of Poland's highest civilian medals and he is admired throughout Germany and Austria. He even counts the president of Romania as a good friend. But power brokers are hardly the epicenter of the rabbi's life.

With a unique sense of humor and a special knack for telling a story, he is also a master of the disarming gesture. The rabbi has been known to be distracted by moths.

One Friday night, a moth was flitting about the window of the Besser dining room during the Shabbos dinner. The candles were glowing, the rich, warm smells of dinner wafted through the room, and the rabbi got up to open the window to let the confused insect outside.

"It looks like the butterfly would rather be out than in," he said.

A guest corrected him: "It isn't a butterfly, it's a moth."

"I know," the rabbi responded with that smile, "but it's Shabbos and I wanted the moth to feel a little better about itself. Everyone should feel better on Shabbos."

All creatures—high and low—get equal treatment.

THE SHTIBEL

Rabbi Besser has a definite destination when he leaves his house at 6:30 every morning. It's the same trip he has made daily for the past fifty years: he crosses the street.

The destination is a brownstone house that, except for the discreet Hebrew lettering over the front door, looks like all the other brownstones on this residential block of Manhattan's Upper West Side. But walking through the front door of that brownstone is like walking through a portal into another era. You could easily be in Eastern Europe a century ago.

At 6:30 in the morning, the rabbi is often the first person to arrive. He goes through the usual ritual of unlocking the door, turning on the lights, and walking up the stairs, perhaps a bit slower than he once did. Sometimes "Doc," his friend and the unofficial caretaker of the building (Doc's day job is cardiology), gets there first and takes care of these mundane details. But the rabbi is happy to do them himself.

The initial observation of a first-time visitor to this brownstone is how unfancy everything is. The first floor contains only a metal coatrack with wire hangers. There's a small sink for washing hands and a bulletin board with various community announcements tacked up in a haphazard way. On the right is the staircase, covered by a frayed and wornout carpet, which leads to the main room on the second floor. It smells a little like the stacks of a university library containing endless shelves of books dating back to the nineteenth century.

At the top of the steps, a plain curtain separates you from the main room of the building. Pulling it back leads to the next surprise: a scene of what appears to be complete disorganization. Prayer books are scattered on various tables, and the chairs and tables are set in what appears to be a completely random way.

Although this is a house of worship, it is unlike most of the thousands of synagogues and churches throughout the United States where pews are placed in strict regimental order, all facing the front. Here the chairs are facing every which way, which seems unavoidable because the floor plan of the brownstone—which is wide, narrow, and then wide again—doesn't lend itself to the usual kind of order.

The differences don't stop there. Practically every inch of wall space is covered with bookshelves bulging with more prayer books: sidurim for daily prayers, special prayer books for holidays, chumashim for Torah readings, and volumes of the Talmud along with even more volumes of commentaries on the Talmud.

There is a small kitchen in the back that looks like it hasn't been updated in forty years, yet still produces delicious lunches for the entire congregation after most Shabbos services.

Technically, the brownstone isn't really a synagogue at all. It's a shtibel.

The shtibel is an invention of the Hasidic movement, which began in Poland in the 1750s. There was tremendous resistance to this new movement from established Judaism at the time because Hasidism altered everything—from the way Jews viewed G-d and life to the way they dressed. Up until then, Judaism had made no alterations—for thousands of uninterrupted years this religion hadn't changed.

Since the general reaction to these changes from mainstream Judaism was hostile, Hasidism was forced to separate itself, and that included the places where they worshiped. In eighteenth-century Poland, where there wasn't a great deal of money and there was a vicious intolerance by non-Jewish Poles, the obvious place to conduct Hasidic services was in someone's apartment (the word *shtibel* means "room").

Later, when the movement overtook all other forms of Judaism in Poland and the reasons for confinement to small spaces no longer applied, Hasidim were comfortable with the smaller venues and continued to gather in their shtibelech (the plural for shtibel).

At the height of the Polish Jewish experience, just before World War II, there were only three large synagogues in Warsaw, but there were more than three hundred shtibelech scattered throughout the city. Sometimes the great rebbes separated groups of men into various shtibelech to avoid conflict. Some were divided by age groups and some for more unusual reasons. In Lodz, there was a shtibel known by the acronym B-B, standing for "bez brody," meaning "without beards." That shtibel was for more modern Hasidim.

Everything in these tightly knit Hasidic communities centered around these small houses of learning where men gathered to pray and study for up to five hours a day, every day. There was nothing fancy or grand about the shtibelech. But what they lacked in size and comfort, they made up for in warmth. A shtibel is much more intimate than a large synagogue.

European shtibelech were second homes where members met each morning for prayers and ended each day with three or four hours of study after dinner. The men would also come together to discuss and solve their personal problems, giving it the feel of a social club.

Problems were presented and debated, and almost always a correlation was drawn from the Talmud. Marriages were given their final approval. Advice was dispensed. Decisions were handed down not unlike those of the Supreme Court. Once the rebbe gave his answer, the matter was decided—"der rebbe hot gezugt!" ("the rebbe has spoken!")—and that was that.

Actually, though, the shtibel is a perfect fit for Rabbi Besser's egalitarian personality. In the great synagogues, the wealthier members get the coveted seats closer to the front, establishing a de facto class system. In the shtibel, a millionaire can sit and study next to a pauper. In fact, it goes one step further. They don't just sit together, they treat each other as equals. The most respected members are not necessarily the wealthiest, but the most learned.

And like a shtibel in prewar Poland, Rabbi Besser's shtibel has taken on his name. Stop almost any Orthodox Jew on the West Side of Manhattan and ask where the Besser shtibel is and you will likely be pointed in the right direction.

After he touches the mezuzah on the door and puts his fingers to his lips, Rabbi Besser heads to the kitchen in the back where he starts a coffeepot. With a cup of weak coffee in hand, he sits down at a long table near the door. There, he opens up a huge volume of the Talmud as two or three other members come in and sit across from him. The morning Talmud class has begun as the rabbi begins to read aloud from the intricate detail of the day's tract.

READING THE TALMUD

There are really two Torahs, and the Talmud is one of them. There is the Torah most people know—the one that is set on scrolls and is the central part of the Jewish religious service. This Torah, the Torah Shebiktav, is also known as the Old Testament to non-Jews. It consists of the Five Books of Moses—Genesis, Exodus, Leviticus, Numbers, and Deuteronomy—along with the nineteen books of the Prophets.

Then there is Torah Shebalpeh—commonly referred to as the Talmud. Unlike the first Torah, which tells the history of G-d's creation and the founding of Judaism, the Talmud is the intricate set of laws and codes of conduct that detail how Jews should live their lives.

The text deals with practically everything a human being will encounter in life. It ranges from ways to deal with a mother-in-law to problems encountered in contractual business agreements, from why certain animals are considered kosher to when to go to war. There are also important discussions about sex. It is, after all, about life and everything that it involves.

But the text is also cumbersome. It lacks the poetry of the Bible. In the morning class, there is some give-and-take,

but for the most part, the rabbi reads and translates, sometimes breaking up the struggle of a particularly difficult passage with a wry remark.

Originally, the Talmud was not supposed to be a written document like Torah Shebiktav. It was passed down
orally from generation to generation. But around the year
150 C.E., one of the most revered rabbis in Jewish history,
Rabbi Judah, also known as Judah the Prince, thought that
this method of passing down these very exacting laws was
not working as an oral transmission—he was afraid the people's minds were becoming weaker. So in those very early
days, Judah the Prince began the difficult task of writing
down the Talmud.

Although the process began in 150 C.E., it wasn't completed until the sixth century—about 450 years later. What
came out of this ordeal is a massive work that has had addi-
tional parts added to it over the centuries.

There are thirty-five parts to the Talmud—we'll call
them volumes. These volumes are made up of blots—or
folios, two pages facing each other. Some volumes have
more blots than others. The shortest volume has only 25
blots. The longest volume of the Talmud—Baba Batra ("the
last volume"), contains 156 blots. In all, there are 2,500 blots
in the Talmud, written mostly in Aramaic—the national language of the Jews before the Babylonian siege of Jerusalem
that has not been a spoken language for over two thousand
years.

A reader's first response to seeing a blot is an inevitable squint. The lettering is a marvel of miniaturization
and invariably leads to the question: How has so much writing been squeezed onto one page?

The main focus is the center of the page where the
original text—the Mishnah—is located. But there is much

A typical half-page of Talmud from the fourth chapter of Menachot which
details the intricate workings of the first and second temples. The Mishnah is at
the center of the page followed by the Babylonian commentary. Rashi's
commentary runs down the coveted inner side to the left of the Mishnah. To
the right of the Mishnah is the Tosafot commentary written by a group of three
hundred scholars led by three of Rashi's grandsons. On the far right is the
commentary of Rabenu Gershon, who lived fifty years before Rashi. The outer
left and right columns are a collection of commentaries edited in the fifteenth
century. At the very bottom is the work of Rabbi Joel Sirkis who lived in
seventeenth-century Poland. Footnotes and references are at the upper right.

more writing that literally surrounds the Mishnah—these are all commentaries and commentaries on the commentaries. The first, known as the Babylonian Commentary because that is where it was written, follows the Mishnah down the middle column. That is followed by perhaps the Talmud's most brilliant commentary written by Rashi (Reb Shlomo Yitzchaki). He lived in the eleventh century in Worms, Germany. What makes Rashi unique is not just his insight, which is vast, but the concise form of his writing. Rashi uses one word where other writers use ten. There are as many as two hundred other scholars who added commentaries between the twelfth and fourteenth centuries.

Rabbi Besser has never been intimidated by the small type or the intricate commentary. He has devoted his life to its study and is convinced that if he keeps studying the text (he has gone through it ten times so far), he will know more. He will understand more. And that will make him a better person.

Asked what he was looking for in all of this writing, he offered a two-word answer: "The truth."

Sitting in the shtibel with the large volume in front of him on a raised lectern, Rabbi Besser looks and sounds more like an elderly law professor helping his students wade through a complex legal text. He makes the detailed writing more manageable with his frequent asides to offer an explanation with a modern analogy. Sometimes, he'll stop to sip from his cup of coffee, which is by now tepid at best.

THE MORNING SERVICE

Meanwhile, as the class proceeds, the shtibel starts to come alive. Between 7 and 7:15 more men of various ages filter in.

Some are dressed in business suits. Some look like they just stepped out of a Gap ad. The only thing distinguishing all of them from other West Siders is that their heads are covered with either yarmulkes or fedoras. A few of the younger men wear baseball caps and carry knapsacks.

As soon as the men get to their seats, they begin the process of quietly putting on their tefillin—the two small boxes with long black straps that contain parchments of written prayers. Then they begin to daven—to pray—as they quietly recite psalms or personal prayers before the actual service commences.

Around 7:15 the rabbi looks up to see the group that has assembled, closes his book, and says simply, "Perhaps we'll stop now and continue tomorrow."

Then he gets up and moves to the forward section in the next room, near the ark that holds the Torah scrolls. He will greet various members as he moves up, often answering a question put to him, sometimes ending the conversation with a play on words, and always with that warm smile.

But when he gets to his chair, the morning prayers—shacharis—begin and for the next thirty minutes there is no kibitzing. When the rabbi davens, his demeanor changes. The smile disappears and he seems to go deep into thought. It's obvious even to the casual observer that this is a man who takes this time very seriously.

THE RABBI AND THE SHTIBEL

Haskel Besser never intended to be a shtibel's rabbi. He wanted to be an orchestra conductor. That was his plan before the war turned the world upside down. His love of classical music is still as strong as ever and his knowledge is astounding. He and his younger son, Naftali, used to play a game when they turned on the car radio, which was always tuned to the classical station. Naftali would check his watch and the Rabbi had to name the composer and the piece of music within six seconds. He rarely lost. Often, he knew the conductor and orchestra as well.

"You always know what mood he is in by the music he listens to," his daughter Debbie observes. "If he is listening to Mahler, you know he is dealing with a difficult issue. If he is listening to Mozart, he is much more relaxed."

Haskel Besser has always been very religious and active in Jewish causes, but, like his father, he did not devote his entire life to study as some Hasidic men do. After the detour in his musical career, he became a businessman. He had trained to become a rabbi and received his smicha (ordination) in British Palestine during World War II, but it is not uncommon for Orthodox Jews to follow this path of study and diverge into other fields. (It is similar to someone who receives a college degree in the United States, but never ends up working in his field of study.)

He became the rabbi of the Upper West Side shul in a roundabout way, but now, after so many years, it seems as if he's always been there.

The shtibel was founded by a group of Hungarian Jews in 1948, predating Rabbi Besser's arrival by four years. In fact, when Rabbi Besser began attending services after he moved into the building across the street in 1952, he was the only member who did not speak Hungarian (he speaks five languages fluently: German, Polish, Hebrew, Yiddish, and English).

Shortly after he became a regular member of the shtibel, he was surprised when the rabbi asked if he would like to become its president.

"I felt very awkward because I was a newcomer there," he recalls. Bear in mind, the shtibel was founded in 1948 and the rabbi started coming in 1952—not exactly a sea of time.

Rabbi Besser became more and more involved in the little shul across the street, first as member, then as its president, and then second counselor to the rabbi.

That changed in 1966 when the long-standing rabbi who led the congregation retired and the search began for a new spiritual leader. Everyone seemed to know the logical choice, but the election was delayed until Rabbi Besser was out of town.

"It was a conspiracy of sorts," he wryly recalls.

Rabbi Besser had gone to Montreal for the celebration of the birth of his first grandchild, a daughter born to his elder son, Shlomo. When he returned, he learned there had been a write-in campaign and he had been elected the new rabbi by an almost unanimous vote.

In characteristic fashion, he declined, but was persuaded to at least think about it. He asked for three days.

"I never wanted to be out in front or have the light shining on me," he says, referring to both his modest nature as well as a Talmudic commentary.

While it's true that the sages suggest one should stay away from the limelight as well as a ruling position—the Torah is very clear that people should walk humbly on earth—the theory according to the rabbi is more specific.

"It really warns against becoming a baal gaava—someone who has too high an opinion of himself, too much pride."

The rabbi has always taken this particular tract seriously. He always returns a compliment with an equal or greater one. He is courteous in all of his actions, whether he's dealing with an influential politician or a bus driver. He will deflect any honors sent his way.

But he found one compelling reason that pushed him to take the position. He knew that as rabbi of the shtibel, he would be forced to study even more than he did already. That was the plus that outweighed the minuses.

The shtibel was clearly aware of his many talents. "There is no one else that has the depth of knowledge—both Jewish and worldly—that Haskel Besser does," says George Klein, a longtime member and a close friend. "Plus, there is that sense of humor and his amazing rapport with children."

So, the rabbi finally agreed to take the position, but on three conditions. First, he would not accept a salary—the one condition the shtibel had no problem accepting. He still jokes that his first condition may have been the reason they chose him. The second caveat was that he did not want to sit at the front—again, not wanting to draw too much attention. On this condition, the members persuaded him to change his mind.

The third condition was that the other members not wait for him to finish his prayers before going on to the next. It is customary for the congregation to wait for the rabbi. Rabbi Besser did not want members who moved at a faster pace to get bored waiting for him. The committee members worked out an unusual compromise on this one, a tacit understanding: they say they don't wait, but they wait anyway.

In the more than thirty years that have passed, the rabbi has grown in stature in the outside world. He has been honored in presidential palaces in foreign capitals. Prime ministers have called seeking his advice. He has had private conversations with world leaders from presidents to the pope. But even with his constant travel and his fame, he always comes back to the small, unpretentious little shtibel on the West Side.

It doesn't matter where he's been or who he has seen. This is home.

But it wasn't always.

Two

KATOWICE

I n order to understand Rabbi Besser, who he is and where he came from, one has to understand Hasidism and how Hasidic Jews differ from Orthodox Jews.

Until the eighteenth century, almost all Jews were Orthodox—the Conservative and Reform movements had not yet begun. And, to put it bluntly, Judaism was not a happy religion. There was a constant sadness in almost every aspect. Even though it took place over seventeen hundred years earlier, Jews still mourned the destruction of the Temple in Jerusalem by the Romans and their exile from Israel.

But in 1736, a charismatic rabbi named Israel ben Eliezer, who lived on the Polish-Ukrainian border, broke away from austere Orthodoxy and created a revolutionary way for Jews to view both G-d and themselves. He saw a people who had replaced happiness and delight with sorrow and grief and it permeated every aspect of their lives. Rabbi ben Eliezer, who became known as the Baal Shem Tov ("Of a Good Reputation"), understood the impact of exile and persecution on generations of Jews.

The Baal Shem Tov strongly disagreed with the despondent interpretation of Judaism and turned everything upside down when he came up with the revolutionary concept that Jews should no longer be sad—they should be happy. He didn't just pull this out of the air—he saw profound reasons to make this turn.

The Baal Shem Tov said that Jews should rejoice and thank G-d for every moment of life. Not only should Jews be thankful for life, but of all the people on earth, they were fortunate to have been given the Torah. He attacked melancholy in all forms with a vengeance. It was melancholy, he said, that caused everything from heartache to ill health. Conversely, he believed that happiness and joy led to healthier lives and a closer relationship to G-d. And he stressed that all Jews, not just the great sages, had the capacity to approach G-d directly.

This may not sound revolutionary in the twenty-first century, but it was unheard of almost three hundred years ago and it did not go over well with the ruling religious elite at the time. The chief opposition came from the rabbinic belief that Judaism had been continuing just fine up until then: Why tinker with something that wasn't broken?

The Baal Shem Tov disagreed and thought a fix was in order. He didn't just change the Jewish outlook. He changed everything—even the most mundane details. His followers differentiated themselves from other Jews in their dress, which they modeled after the noblemen of their day, as well as their prayers and songs, which were more fervent. The synagogue was eventually replaced by the shtibel. But in some ways these were just cosmetic changes. The most salient difference from mainstream Judaism came in the great joy Hasids found in every single aspect of their lives, from the way they approached Shabbos and holidays to the way they dealt with their children. The Torah, they believed, was a treasure, not a burden, given directly by G-d to Jews. G-d was everywhere, even in the commonplace: a tree, an insect, everything was part of G-d's wonderful plan in His creation of the world.

"Hasidim," according to Rabbi Besser, "are more religious because they want to be, not because they are forced to be."

The difference between an Orthodox Jew and a Hasidic Jew can be as simple as finding a ten-dollar bill on the sidewalk.

The Talmud says that if you find money and you did not see who dropped it, it's yours. That's because the previous owner has no way of proving that the money belonged to him, since all ten-dollar bills look alike.

However, Rabbi Besser has been to Hasidic shuls where an entire wall is covered with notices that tell of money found at a certain location at a certain time, in attempts to find the person who lost it.

"The finders, by law, are not obligated to do this," he explains. "But they want to make the extra effort by going beyond their duty to do the right thing. In this way they are honoring G-d."

The students of the Ba'al Shem Tov branched out across Poland in the late eighteenth century, spreading this message and forming their own sects, which quickly took on dynastic characteristics. Leadership was passed down from father to son. If there was no son, a son-in-law was appointed to be the rebbe.

The dynasties were named after the towns where they lived—Sochaczev, Radomsk, Belz, Bobov, Biala, and others.

Although these rebbes had birth names, they were more commonly known by their dynastic names. So, the twentieth-century rabbi, Menachem Schneerson, was better known as the Lubavitch Rebbe, and Rabbi Shlomo Halberstam was usually referred to as the Bobov Rebbe.

These rebbes ruled with brilliance and insight. They not only answered the mundane questions, but were also the ambassadors for their communities to the non-Jewish world. This often required the greatest diplomatic skills, given the animosity of the outside world toward Jews.

It is really no surprise that this movement caught fire. Happiness is profoundly more attractive to the average person than grief. With the idea that the joyful can better achieve purity, the Baal Shem Tov taught people they could find paradise on earth while studying Torah and keeping the Sabbath.

One of the classic Hasidic writers, Rabbi Levi Yitzhak, who lived in Berditchev in the early nineteenth century, explained how the concept of joy over sorrow transformed the lives of Jews.

"A Hasid prays, studies, and lives in exaltation. One can see the fire in his every feature, his speech, his bearing. In the new light that came from the Baal Shem's fire, the pressures of daily life no longer encumbered them. People made of sighs and tears were remade into a people of awe and joy."

Ironically, just before its crushing end Hasidism experienced its golden age. Following World War I, the Treaty of Versailles forced Poland to adopt civil liberties for all minorities. With government-sponsored and Church-supported anti-Semitism put in check for a brief time, Hasidic dynasties flourished. By 1939, there were three and a half million Jews, almost 10 percent of the total Polish population.

Haskel Besser was born right in the middle of this golden age on the twenty-ninth day of Shevat, February 14, 1923. His father was Naftali Besser, a highly successful, young Hasidic banker. Naftali and his wife, Frometta Besser, were descended from long-standing Hasidic families (they were actually first cousins—their fathers were brothers). But there was one thing that differentiated them from other Hasidim—they were both very modern.

While their world revolved around their religion, they also read newspapers and contemporary literature, listened to classical music, and followed world events closely. Mrs. Besser was quite fond of the theater and opera and attended plays and concerts regularly (usually with her sister-in-law, Mania, Naftali's sister and Frometta's closest friend).

The Bessers lived in the city of Katowice, Poland. They were devoted followers of one of the great Hasidic dynasties—the Radomskers. Naftali was particularly close to its leader, the Radomsker Rebbe, Shlomo Rabinowitz, serving as one of his principal advisers.

As a sign of devotion and respect and, perhaps, hopeful that their newborn son would follow the example of his namesake, the Bessers named their new son after the Radomsker Rebbe's late father, the previous Radomsker Rebbe, Haskel Rabinowitz.

Ashkenazic Jews never name a child after someone still alive. By naming this new life after someone who has died, parents are honoring the deceased as well as keeping their memory alive. There are also more mystical factors at play. Now that he has seen as much as he has, Rabbi Besser insists that he has watched children actually show personality traits of the person they are named after. All the more reason, according to the rabbi, to make sure it's a good name.

There is not a lot known about Haskel Rabinowitz. Like his father before him and his son after, the rebbe led many thousands of devoted followers until his death in 1911. He was certainly very pious and a greatly admired rebbe, but that could be said about almost every Hasidic rebbe. He carried on the traditions of Hasidism, as other rebbes did. But there is one characteristic that, for anyone who knows Rabbi Besser, is striking: the late Radomsker Rebbe was a very humble leader. Haskel Rabinowitz did not desire or crave attention—a trait that would show itself in his namesake.

Haskel's father, Naftali, made a name for himself as well as a great fortune at a very early age. He founded a bank in 1920, Yoroslowski & Company, when he was twenty-four years old. There were branches in Poland and Germany and, although the Bessers lived in Katowice, he traveled during the week to all of the offices—yet he was always back home for Shabbos. Traveling for work was not unusual. But what was unusual for that time was Naftali's traveling companion: his wife, Frometta. Although she worked with Naftali, watching over his bookkeeping, she managed to also run a rather unique home.

HOME LIFE

The Besser home was really a social center—a focal point for the entire community. In Hebrew, it is called hachnesos orchim—a home where any Jew will always be welcome. On any given Shabbos, there could be forty people at the dining table. Visitors could get advice, borrow money, or even use the address to pick up their mail. The Besser residence in Katowice was an elegant apartment at 3 Dyrek-

Eight-year-old Haskel Besser listening to music in Kudova, Germany, 1931, with Reisel Rabinowitz, the only child of the Radomsker Rebbe. *(Family photograph)*

Haskel Besser's father, Naftali *(left),* riding in an open convertible with the Radomsker rebbe *(hat in hand)* at a spa in Luhacovice, Czechoslavkia, in the summer of 1934. *(Family photograph)*

The Radomsker rebbe *(second from left)* surrounded by his followers
on a walk in Krynica, Poland, in 1936. Naftali Besser is the tall man
to his right. The young boy in front of Naftali is Haskel's cousin,
Israel Chaim, who would die at the hands of the Nazis shortly after
his bar mitzvah. *(Family photograph)*

cyjna Street. It was in the center of town, just three blocks
from the main train station. On one end of the block was
the great Monopol Hotel, where, from his bed, Haskel
could hear the orchestra playing late into the night in the
summer. At the opposite end of the street was the great state
theater, where Mrs. Besser went to see her beloved sym-
phonies and Shakespeare.

In the apartment's front hallway, there were large book-
cases filled with what were considered the "profane" books:
Tolstoy, Shakespeare, Schiller, and Goethe. They were
never mixed with the religious volumes, which were kept
in a different room altogether. But even this seemingly

small gesture to modernity was highly unusual for a Hasidic family in this era. Most had only religious texts.

Although they worked together and shared a generous spirit, Naftali and Frometta were also different. His circle was Hasidic. She was more social. Frometta had many more friends than her husband. His free time was spent with the rebbe. She went to the theater. Naftali studied the Torah. Under Frometta's eye, and with the help of a cook, a maid, and a governess, the house ran with clockwork precision.

Although Katowice was technically in Poland, the majority of the population was ethnic German. The Treaty of Versailles left it under German control, but the city was returned to Poland in 1921 after violent Polish uprisings. The German influence, however, never went away. The civil government was German, as was the city's spoken language, as it had been for the previous 180 years.

The Besser home was quite German in its orderliness and precise schedule.

"It was very regimented. You knew what soup there would be on Monday, what soup on Tuesday—it never changed."

Thursday—the day before Shabbos—was washday.

On Sundays the table grew miraculously to accommodate even more people than on Shabbos: there could be as many as sixty guests in the home.

Besides the strangers who came and went, the Besser home was filled with an odd cast of permanent characters worthy of a Broadway play. There was, of course, the immediate family (Naftali, Frometta, Haskel, and his two siblings, Rosa, his older sister, and Akiva, his younger brother), and there were regulars who joined the family at dinner every night. Both of Haskel's tutors had a place at the table—the more pious teacher who taught Haskel the Gemara (religious studies) and the other teacher, a left-winger, who taught him modern Hebrew. The two teachers, at odds over politics and religion, never even acknowledged each other.

"My mother's niece and nephew were also there every night, along with a friend, Hendel Pachter. He was just there—I'm not sure why. He stuck to us."

There was also the shamos (the caretaker) of the shul and his son. Haskel's maternal grandparents stayed with them every Shabbos and all holidays.

On Saturday afternoons, after the Shabbos services and lunch, Naftali would lead a group of around twenty-five people on a walk to Kosciuszko Park. Naftali was the natural leader and guided the conversations. The topics were wide-ranging, from the parsha (Torah reading) of the week to politics (both Jewish and non-Jewish) to stories about the world before the Great War. Haskel would walk by his father's side, very proud that of all the fathers to have in the world, this one was his.

Shabbos in the Besser home was a model of what this holy day should be. A devout feeling came over the inhabitants, the discussions honored G-d, and the intellectual atmosphere was invigorating. It was strikingly similar to the home the rabbi and his wife created years later in Manhattan. The warmth and openness are there, strangers are welcome and always made to feel they are honoring the family by being there—instead of the other way around—another Hasidic practice.

Haskel's sister, Rosa, went to the German public school. Before Haskel was old enough to go to school himself, he would pick her up with his governess every day. Even at the age of three or four, young Haskel didn't waste time. While he waited for her in the hallways, he learned

German history by studying the pictures of the German kings and emperors hanging on the walls.

"I loved those pictures," Rabbi Besser remembers. "They were beautifully painted."

Katowice's German influence left its mark on Haskel. He admired that country for its culture, its history, and, especially, its modern accomplishments. Rabbi Besser still marvels at his first trip to Berlin in 1929. Through the eyes of a six-year-old boy, it was a magical place. He was mesmerized by the city's subway system and its art deco airport. "I could have spent hours just watching the planes take off and land at Tempelhof airport."

Germany, with its modern inventions, was the future's promise. As a perceptive small boy, Haskel understood that it was light-years ahead of his native Poland.

Katowice was the capital of Upper Silesia, a rich industrial city in the middle of a great mining range. When Haskel was a child and traveled by train at night, he remembers looking out, fascinated by the bright orange-and-yellow glow from the blast furnaces of the foundries on the outskirts of the city.

The streets of Katowice were cleaner than in other Polish cities. Store shelves were well stocked. Everything seemed to work there—something that was not always the case in Poland. Because it was also a wealthy city, the theater just down the street from the Bessers was one of the largest in the country.

The Jews who lived in Katowice (about 10 percent of the total population) were also different from Jews elsewhere in Poland. They dressed more formally, like the Jews of Frankfurt or Berlin. After Yiddish, Rabbi Besser's second language was German, not Polish. There was even a law in Katowice that every child had to have a German name.

So when Frometta registered him with the town hall shortly after his birth, the officials offered her two choices (Haskel was a Jewish name and would not suffice). Rabbi Besser was never happy with the one she picked, Oswald.

"One of the fascist leaders in England was named Oswald," he would later explain. Then, with classic understatement, he adds, "There was another Oswald after that who was not so nice." There was really no good way out of this one: the only other choice offered to his mother was "Heinrich," a name made infamous fifteen years later by Heinrich Himmler, the head of the SS and one of Hitler's top aides.

But except for a rare piece of mail, no one calls him Oswald. His grandchildren and great-grandchildren call him saba (grandfather in Yiddish and Hebrew), his wife and a few close friends call him by his Yiddish name, Haskel. Everyone else, Jewish and non-Jewish, just calls him rabbi.

Young Haskel was educated first by tutors and then in yeshivas. At home, he didn't just read religious and nonreligious books, he devoured them. And he loved listening to classical music. Occasionally he accompanied his mother to the theater and concerts. This sparked his lifelong love of music.

As a child, he played with non-Jewish friends. There were newspapers and magazines in the house. They even went to movies. "That would never have happened if I hadn't been born in Katowice." Like the Bessers, many of the Jews of Katowice were more modern than the Jews in other Polish cities. And this set a pattern that would continue throughout his life. There has never been a question about Rabbi Besser's religious credentials. But what has set him apart is his openness to modern ideas. "We found out that you could be dressed in a modern way and understand the secular world and still be very religious."

For Rabbi Besser, this has never been a conflict. He has always felt perfectly comfortable in both worlds, as long as the "outside" world allowed him to practice his Hasidism.

"I think I always had an open mind," he says, looking back. "Jews or non-Jews—it didn't matter. I enjoyed meeting people and the people I met in those years were good people. I think I'm still affected by these memories, because I cannot believe the way some people have painted *all* Germans as anti-Semites. Not the people I knew."

He admits he doesn't know how these people behaved during the war. "They could have been SS," he says. "That's really beside the point. The real question is, how could people who were so normal, so nice, be turned into savages? This I have not yet answered. But to say they were anti-Semitic from the beginning just does not fit with what I remember."

As for the theory that Hitler only unleashed Germany's true national character, Rabbi Besser disagrees with that as well.

"I am convinced that Hitler and his gang tried for years to turn Jews into abnormal human beings . . . parasites who should be extinguished without any remorse. The same way you would kill a louse. I'm pretty sure it would be easy to teach any nation this—even countries that have been very good to Jews. After two or three years of injecting such venom into a national character, people's views can change."

Berlin was a second home to Haskel Besser. Naftali Besser had three brothers who lived there and Mrs. Besser had a brother there as well. Besides his business, Naftali also owned property there. In the summers, the families vacationed in German spas in the old European tradition. It was not unusual for many people to spend two months, July and

August, away from the cities. The wealthier families went to international resorts like Baden Baden, St. Moritz, or Carlsbad in Czechoslovakia. Famous Hasidic rebbes came to these same spas with thousands of their followers. These gatherings were similar to religious conventions—one of the rare times all of the Hasidic rebbes came together. The rabbi looks back on these summers with great affection.

When the international depression began in 1929, the Besser home seemed immune from the world's economic woes. Naftali did lose a great deal of money when a major German financial institution, the Dresdner Bank, failed. But the family always had more than enough. And throughout the thirties, the door of the Besser home was always open.

So here was a wealthy, happy, modern Hasidic family. The outlook for young Haskel was good. He was bright and inquisitive. His family adored him and he was already known as an exceptional child by some of the most important rebbes in the country.

His future was bright—or at least it should have been.

Three

Flight

By the time Haskel Besser was only ten years old, in 1933, he knew his world had changed.

"I could smell it," he remembers. "I watched the German elections of 1929 and 1930. I studied maps. And I could see the anti-Jewish propaganda was working."

In January 1933, two weeks before Hitler became the chancellor of Germany, Haskel was walking down a Berlin street with one of his uncles. Suddenly three trucks rounded the corner filled with brownshirted thugs wielding baseball bats, looking for Jews. His uncle quickly grabbed his arm and pulled him into a building where they hid until the trucks passed. Then, just weeks after Hitler came to power, a gentile accosted Naftali in his bank in Hindenburg.

"Someone threw a telephone at his head," recalls the rabbi. But it wasn't just any someone. The man was Naftali's business partner and one of his closest friends for over a decade. That was all it took. Unlike so many other Jews, Naftali understood that something profound had overtaken the German psyche and the lives of Jews were going to get much worse. This was not, in his mind, just a passing phase.

Naftali Besser quickly liquidated all of his businesses in Germany, although he held on to his real estate—six buildings in Berlin—a decision that would bring Haskel back to that country many years later.

"I read the Nuremberg laws; I saw the parades, which were colossal. I listened to all of Hitler's speeches," the rabbi remembers. "I couldn't help listening. Even though what I heard made me very uncomfortable, I was fascinated. He was a very powerful speaker."

Although Naftali understood it was no longer safe to be a Jew in Germany, his brothers did not. "I once asked one of my uncles how he could continue to live in Germany," recalls the rabbi, "especially since he wore a beard and looked so obviously Jewish." His uncle insisted he felt safer in Berlin at midnight than he did in Poland at noon. That was not an uncommon thought at that time. Poland, along with Russia, had always been considered the epicenters of anti-Semitism in Europe and this belief was backed by history.

Oddly, when Haskel's extended family had the chance to change their citizenship, they did not. Fifteen years earlier, the kaiser offered Naftali's older brother, Moishe, and his entire family German citizenship as a reward for exceptional work during World War I. German citizenship certainly seemed safer than Polish for a Jew. But rather than simply accepting the kaiser's offer, Naftali and his brothers first asked the Radomsker Rebbe for his opinion—as they did with every important decision. To their surprise, the rebbe advised *against* it. At the time, the advice, which they followed, may not have appeared to make sense. But the rebbe understood that if things ever changed in Germany, a religious Jew would have greater protection living there as a

foreigner than a native subject to German laws. He understood that Germans always followed the law. The rebbe's
prescience predated anyone's awareness of Hitler.

The rebbe was right. From 1933 until 1938, foreign
Jews lived under the protection of their embassies. Moishe,
the only brother to go against the rebbe's recommendation
and take German citizenship, was subject to the Nuremberg
laws and other increasingly draconian racial decrees.

"Immediately after Hitler became chancellor, Germany's sense of law and order more or less continued. At
first, the only people he actually killed were in his own
party," recalls the rabbi. "Though Jews were arrested and
sent to concentration camps, the mass killings did not occur
during those early years. Germany was still very sensitive to
international opinion."

All of that changed in 1938 and the catalyst seemed to
be Germany's annexation of Austria. Soon after the Anschluss, all of the pent-up venom against Jews in Austria
came flooding out. "After this, the German Nazis found out
that you could beat up Jews and nothing happened," observes the rabbi. "There really wasn't much of an outcry
from world leaders."

The Anschluss took place around the Jewish holiday of
Purim and Rabbi Besser remembers how one guest at the
family's dinner had a very sobering impact on the usually
jolly observance of this holiday. "He had escaped from Vienna where he witnessed the reaction of the Austrians in
the streets. It was the first time we had actually heard that
Jews were being killed." To this day, Purim always reminds
the rabbi of this event and the chilling effect the story had
on his family and everyone at the table.

KRISTALLNACHT

Several months later, in the late summer of 1938, one of Haskel's uncles, David Koschitski, was arrested in Berlin and charged with holding dollars and other currency abroad. He was jailed for two months by the Gestapo but finally released after it became apparent that he was innocent.

But just a few days after he returned home, Haskel's uncle was summoned back to police headquarters. This time, he brought along a small bag with his prayer shawl, tefillin, soap, and a toothbrush, expecting another long stay. The same officer who had interrogated him asked him to sit down.

"Listen," the officer told him, "it is now nine-twenty in the morning. At one twenty-eight this afternoon there is an express train leaving for Poland. I would like you to pack whatever you can, round up your family and your friends, and be on that train."

"What does this mean?" his uncle inquired.

"Please don't ask me," the officer implored. "I can't tell you any more. Just take whatever you can and tell all your friends the same thing."

Rabbi Besser remembers a phone call that night from his uncle, telling them they had just arrived in Poland. This was on a Thursday. The next day, Germany expelled every Jew who had originally come from Poland—even though some had lived in Germany for decades. Many young adults were born there and had never lived anyplace else. This great mass of humanity was simply dumped at the border in Zbaszyn. There they sat with whatever they could carry, stranded for days. The Germans didn't want them. The Poles didn't want them. No government on the face of the earth wanted them—a point not lost on Zionists.

This action by Hitler inadvertently sparked the next great event of that period. Among the twenty-five thousand Jews who were kicked out of the country was a family named Greenspan. Their seventeen-year-old son, Herschel, lived in Paris at the time and was so incensed by the treatment of his family that he walked into the German embassy in Paris the next day and shot the attaché. Ironically, the attaché Greenspan killed, named von Rath, was more sympathetic to his plight than many other Germans.

The irony became even crueler. Hitler used von Rath's death as the excuse for unleashing a national pogrom throughout Germany and Austria—Kristallnacht. In a vicious and violent campaign coordinated through local Gestapo offices, more than one thousand synagogues were burned to the ground on November 9 and 10, 1938. Jewish-owned businesses were sacked. Jews were arrested, beaten, and killed. Perhaps even worse than the violence was the world reaction. It was mute. The Germans realized they now had a free hand regarding the treatment of Jews.

Rabbi Besser remembers reading about the shooting of von Rath by Greenspan and having a sense of foreboding. He understood that the Germans would use this event as a pretext to hurt the general Jewish population. Most of the news of Kristallnacht was carried in the Jewish press. Polish newspapers did not cover the story to any great extent. "When they did," recalls Rabbi Besser, "it was with a sense of schadenfreude."

Looking back on how that particular Gestapo officer helped his uncle, Rabbi Besser has often wondered why this aid came from such unusual quarters. "After interrogating someone for two months, you get to know that person. I think he saw my uncle was a good, honest man. So perhaps when the officer heard what was about to happen, he thought, 'Let me help this man as a way of apologizing for the previous two months.' They were so disciplined and obedient to the law, this Gestapo officer could have said this is the law and that's that. Instead, the officer reached beyond his national character and tried to help. In fact, he went against orders and in doing so, he went even further against character."

At the same time, the ugly mood in Germany quickly spread across the border. Shortly after Kristallnacht, Haskel came in from school one afternoon to find the local police tearing his home apart. One officer took out his gun and searched Haskel for weapons. Of course, the officer found none. But Haskel did have something that turned out to be equally incriminating. He was carrying photographs of his sister's wedding. Rosa had recently married Mordechai Abramczyk in a typically large Hasidic wedding.

"Very nice wedding," the policeman noted. "How much did it cost?"

Fifteen-year-old Haskel had no idea.

That turned out to be all the proof the Polish officer needed. There was a huge wedding that, according to the officer, must have cost a fortune—clearly the Bessers had to be breaking some law.

That wasn't the only charge as a result of that raid. The police found a crystal set that Haskel built. All radios had to be registered and he was in possession of an unregistered radio. The family had a permit for the larger radio in the living room, but there was no permit for the crystal set. Later in court, Haskel tried to explain he had no radio permit because this wasn't a radio, it was a crystal set. It didn't matter. He was fined.

Naftali was taken to jail and whoever came to the apartment over the next day (around twenty-five people)

was arrested as well. Naftali was held for three weeks, until
the police found he had done nothing illegal.

But that's all it took for Naftali. It may have seemed to
some an impetuous reaction but, once again, he grasped the
seriousness of the situation. The first thing he did was move
his family to Lodz, which was the second-largest Jewish city in
Poland. Then, something happened that would ultimately
seal the Besser family's fate: Naftali lost his passport on a
train. He went to the police to report the loss and shortly
after that, a threatening letter arrived. It was written in German and read: "I have your passport. If you go to the police
again, the lives of your wife and children will be in danger."

Luckily, Naftali had a second passport from another
country. Two years earlier, on a trip to Vienna, a friend mentioned that Naftali was eligible for Austrian citizenship because he was born in Szczakowa, which was then part of the
Austro-Hungarian Empire. He had forgotten about that second passport, until he found it while looking through a
drawer for some sort of identification. But the story is in-
dicative of how Jews never really felt completely safe in Europe, no matter how honest they were, how rich or
powerful. If there was an opportunity to get a second passport, it made sense—just in case.

The Polish authorities continued to hound Naftali over
taxes, accusing him of failing to report income based on the
pictures of his daughter's wedding. They assessed a huge tax
on him, retroactive not just from the wedding date, but for
the past ten years. Between the false tax accusations and the
missing passport, Naftali had had enough and he came up
with a plan.

He left for Palestine with his Austrian passport and a
tourist visa. Within one week, a letter arrived from Tel Aviv
and the family's future was decided.

My dear wife and children:

I have now been here for six hours. Six hours since I arrived in Palestine. Let me tell you there is no coming back. I'll never come back. Whoever stays in Poland is either stupid or crazy.

I have not breathed such fresh and free air since before the World War. This is the country to be in. I have retained a lawyer and have already started the process of securing your emigration papers.

This was in February 1939. In May, Mrs. Besser along with her younger son, Akiva, left to join Naftali. There was actually a flight from Warsaw to Tel Aviv with one stop in Bucharest. The entire trip took only six hours. Six hours from Poland in 1939 to Palestine, an incredibly short amount of time that took them from persecution and death to freedom and life.

Haskel brought his mother and young brother to the airport. "I was fascinated by the way they boarded the plane. When you checked in, they not only weighed the luggage, but the passenger stood on the scale as well. If you were skinny, you could take more."

The Bessers' daughter remained in Poland with her new husband. Sixteen-year-old Haskel stayed behind to liquidate the family's affairs. Naftali had obtained certificates of entry to Palestine for all of them. These certificates were worth more than gold. Jews could still leave Poland, that wasn't the problem. Finding a country that would accept them was another story. One day, Haskel went into a store where he was recognized as someone who had a *certificate*. "Suddenly, there were twenty-five people surrounding me," he remembers. "They all wanted to see it, to touch it. They understood that such a piece of paper could mean life."

As that fateful summer wore on, the news became more ominous. Hitler started accusing the Poles of atrocities against ethnic Germans—a tactic he had used before he took over other countries. Haskel and one of his uncles decided to leave for Palestine on September 6 by train from Warsaw and then by boat from Constanza. Haskel booked passage and tried to get as much done as he could.

But on August 22, when he was staying at his sister's home in Sosnowiec for a cousin's wedding, he heard a radio report that Moscow had signed a nonaggression pact with Berlin.

"It was eight forty-five in the evening—I even remember the time. This immediately sent up a red flag—it meant war was imminent." The next day, Haskel called his travel agent, a clever man named Mr. Zaide, and asked to change his visa and ticket. The soonest available departure was on August 28.

"I spent Shabbos, August 25, at my sister's home, where I witnessed a great panic in the streets. All day and night, people were running east—away from the German border—taking their belongings on wagons. It was a pathetic sight.

"My grandparents had also come from Oswiciem to Sosnowiec for the wedding." He remembers saying good-bye. "That was the last time I saw them."

These final good-byes would be repeated many times over the next two days.

On Sunday, August 26, Haskel went to Lodz and was surprised to find that the Radomsker Rebbe was there as well. The rebbe had left Krynica, where he had been spending the summer.

"On Monday, before I left for Warsaw where I was to meet the travel agent at the British embassy, I went to see the rebbe. Some of his most important followers were also in the room."

This group of men was standing over a table looking at a map of Poland when Haskel walked in. The owner of the apartment, Mr. Stahl, looked up and asked: "Haskel, you are supposedly an expert in geography. What's your advice? Where's the safest place to go?"

Even with events spinning out of control around them, Haskel was still very aware of his station vis-à-vis this very important man.

"I felt very honored that as a sixteen-year-old boy, I was asked to advise the rebbe.

"It's important to remember that nobody expected the German blitzkrieg to overrun Poland in just two weeks. We knew the German Army was strong, but Poland had over two million men in its army. They had tanks, artillery, and an air force. So to be two hundred or three hundred kilometers from the German border should have been relatively safe. Therefore, I recommended that the rebbe go to the southeast, near Luck or Kowel, which normally would give him plenty of time before the Germans would get there.

"Of course, nobody predicted that Russia would stab Poland in the back and occupy the eastern half of the country, including these two cities."

One of the rebbe's aides asked Haskel about the flight his mother took to Palestine three months earlier.

"I told them there were two flights a week—Monday night and Friday night. Since we were speaking on Monday, it was already too late for that evening's flight since there were no visas."

Another gentleman in the room suggested that although Friday was Shabbos and any kind of travel was strictly forbidden, perhaps because of the emergency situation—the rabbi could make an exception. It was at this point that the Radomsker Rebbe cut everyone off with a prophetic statement: "What will happen to three million Jews will happen to me. I'm not running away."

"Those are some of the last words I heard from him. The rebbe wished me success in my travels and we said good-bye. I never saw him again.

"When I left the apartment I met another very important rebbe, the Sochatshever Rebbe, who was coming into the building. He was also later killed."

This is a watershed moment in Haskel Besser's life, but of course he didn't understand its full significance at the time. This moment also characterized the thinking of many people on the eve of the war. The actions people took to save themselves from danger were based on their experience in the previous war with Germany. Although it was horrific and huge numbers of soldiers were killed, there was no wholesale slaughter of civilian populations. It was a long, drawn-out military affair with very little movement. Just twenty years later, this framework was already completely out-of-date. But almost no one understood this.

The next day, Tuesday, August 29, there was another hurdle, which seemed insurmountable. Haskel went to Warsaw to pick up his visa and Romanian transit papers. But when he opened the newspapers, he was devastated to see that all foreign consulates were closed and would not issue any more visas. He was trapped.

"My travel agent met me and said, 'Don't despair.' He still had a way, but he needed money—a lot of money—to *persuade* the staff of the consulate to work under the table. And I had almost no money."

Haskel had to come up with cash in a hurry. In the midst of the war panic, this wasn't a simple task. He first went to the home of one of Naftali's friends in Warsaw, Rabbi Ehrlich. There he placed a call to his sister in Sosnowiec. Unfortunately, a call that normally took one minute to connect now took hours. The call he placed at 7 P.M. finally connected at 3 A.M.

But Haskel's sister had recently moved into a new apartment and her telephone hadn't been installed. He called the home of her father-in-law and asked if someone would pass along his urgent request for a large sum of money, needed by noon that day.

There was one train that left Sosnowiec at 6:30 A.M. and arrived in Warsaw four hours later. At 10:30 that morning, Haskel was anxiously waiting in Warsaw's main depot as he watched the passengers walk off the train. Finally, in the crowd, he saw his sister and brother-in-law. From that moment, a frantic rush began. They passed along the cash to the travel agent, who obtained the visas and train tickets.

"I told my brother-in-law that I had no tefillin because I left them in Lodz. So on the way to the train, the car stopped twice, first to buy tefillin and then a raincoat. I remember the salesman's surprise—I didn't even have time to try it on. When we arrived at the station, the train had already started to move when I jumped on board."

Haskel was far from safe. Boarding the train in Warsaw was only the first step in a long and frightening journey. The train was bound for Lwow and then Constanta, a port in Romania. Haskel went to the second-class car. When he entered the compartment, he was surprised to see that the only other passenger was a priest. When the conductor came in to check the tickets, both he and the priest noticed that Haskel's ticket was not the normal piece of paper, but a booklet, which meant he was traveling further.

After a while, the priest said, "So you are going to all the way to Constanta."

"Yes," Haskel replied. "I am traveling to the port, where I will take a boat to Palestine."

"Well," said the priest, clearly recognizing that Haskel was Jewish, "the situation is very grave in Palestine."

In 1936, Arab leaders had unleashed what would be three years of attacks against the Jews. Finally in 1938, a small minority of Jews decided to reply in kind.

"It's terrible," the priest continued, "when the Jewish bombs kill innocent Arabs."

"You're referring to the bomb in Haifa where twenty Arabs were killed?" Haskel asked.

"Yes," the priest responded.

"It is always a tragedy when innocent civilians who are not involved are killed," said Haskel.

With that, their conversation ended. Haskel went back to his book and the priest went back to his newspaper. The two sat quietly for an hour until the train stopped at a station called Skarzysko, which was filled with young men—perhaps two or three thousand. Poland was mobilizing its armed forces.

The small compartment was suddenly filled with young men—some in uniform and most smelling of liquor. Seeing a young Jew sitting there in the compartment, some of the soldiers began to get angry.

"Hey," said one of them, "there's a Jew-boy sitting here."

"Where are you going?" asked another.

"He's not going to the army," another taunted.

"No, it doesn't look like he's joining us," said the first.

The situation quickly turned more threatening.

"I think we should throw him out."

Three or four of them started moving toward Haskel. Another opened the window. The train was traveling at 60 miles an hour.

"I have no doubt at all that they would have thrown me out the window without hesitation," the rabbi recalls.

He immediately broke into a cold sweat. Haskel thought of pulling the emergency cord but it was on the other side of the car.

Suddenly, in a deep voice, the priest started to shout: "Where's the conductor? Where's the conductor?"

And soon everyone started to shout: "Conductor! Conductor!"

The conductor came through the mob and asked what was happening. He was told that the priest wanted him.

"What is it, Father?" the conductor asked.

"Are all of these people holding second-class tickets?" the priest asked him.

"Of course not. They have no tickets. They're going to the army," the conductor told the priest.

"Well, let them go to the third class where they belong. Not our compartment," the priest told him.

"Please, Father," the conductor implored. "There is nowhere else to go."

But what the priest requested, the conductor delivered. They all left the compartment and the priest closed the curtains. Then he looked at Haskel and said: "Someone who is against the shedding of innocent blood, I will not let his blood be shed."

After many delays, the train finally arrived in Lwow. But then there was an announcement: "Attention all passengers. Because of the imminent war situation, all train service is suspended. All passengers must leave the train."

"I went down the steps and left the train like everyone else," Rabbi Besser recalls. "But I was bewildered. I had only one pound and four dollars in my wallet along with the train and boat tickets."

He was still a hundred miles from the border.

"Suddenly God gave me an idea. Our train had been an international train. It traveled from Paris to Berlin to Warsaw to Bucharest."

Haskel went up to one of the officials and asked where these international trains were headed.

"We're sending them back to the nearest borders," he replied.

Haskel asked if he could board one of these trains, and the official said no. But as soon as the conductor was out of sight, Haskel tried one of the doors. It opened and he went inside and settled in the corner of the empty car where he could not be seen from the outside.

Soon, the train started up and traveled for about three hours without making any stops, until it suddenly came to an abrupt halt. It turned out that the train was headed straight to the Polish-Romanian border. But they were still on the Polish side of that border, just short of his next destination.

Suddenly, a border guard entered the train and was startled to see Haskel inside.

"Who are you?" he demanded. "Where are you going?"

"I'm going to Romania," Haskel answered.

"Do you have a passport?" the guard asked.

"Of course," he answered.

When the guard looked at the picture, he asked: "Who is this?"

"That's me," he replied.

"No, that's not you," shouted the conductor. "You are a coward. You are running away because of the war. You know

Haskel Besser's passport photo used during his escape from
Poland on September 1, 1939. *(Family photograph)*

what we do with traitors?" the guard asked. "We make it very quick. We don't have time for trials. I'm going to get the police and that will be the end of you."

Luckily, the table next to the seat happened to be extended. It afforded the guard an opportunity for a dramatic gesture and he slammed the passport on the table with a loud crash instead of taking it with him.

"I don't know why he didn't take it," the rabbi recalls many years later. "He could have taken it very easily and that would have been the end. He probably just wasn't thinking."

The guard went out to find the police. But the engineer, who assumed there was no one on the train, started up the train and it began to move. It didn't move far, perhaps only one hundred yards. But that was enough. It was now on Romanian soil.

Haskel got off the train near a busy station and two Romanian officials in elegant uniforms began to speak to him. He couldn't understand them, but suddenly another Jewish man appeared and told him in Yiddish: "They want to see your Romanian visa."

Haskel showed it to them, and they spoke again.

"It's not valid," the translator informed him.

"But it is valid," Haskel argued.

"No," said the translator. "When they say it's not valid, that means they want money. Do you have any money?"

He gave the guard a dollar and magically the visa was valid again. When Haskel boarded the train, it happened again. The conductor told him the ticket was not valid. By law he was allowed to take out four U.S. dollars and one British pound, but his money was quickly running out.

Haskel hadn't eaten for a long time. Once again, luck prevailed. It was September, harvesttime, the train to Constanta was a local train, and farmers were desperate to sell their produce at each station (it was a short season). Melons and apples were plentiful and cheap. Haskel was able to eat.

But even after the harrowing trip and his arrival in Constanta, there was still one last obstacle. The boat to Palestine had already left. About three hundred Jews waited on the dock. Because the original ship, the *Besarabia,* which sailed two days earlier, was overfilled, part of the overflow was put on another boat, the *Romania,* which sailed the day before. But with the port overflowing with Jews, the *Romania* was called back to pick them up. Before the boat touched the pier, Haskel saw two people onboard waving at him.

"They were my uncles—David and Rachmil—two of my father's brothers."

Before he could enter the boat, he was told his boat ticket was not valid. Haskel parted with his last dollar. With that, this sixteen-year-old Jewish boy boarded a boat that took him from Europe on September 1, 1939. By the time he boarded the boat, just before Shabbos, seventeen cities in Poland had already been bombed.

FOUR

OUR HEARTS
WERE BLEEDING

The SS *Romania* was once a luxury ship fitted for 250, and it now carried more than 700 passengers. People and baggage were everywhere. It wasn't comfortable, but that hardly mattered. Haskel Besser was on a ship that was steaming away from Europe.

He spent the four-day journey on the deck. There was plenty of fresh air, but the deck was hosed down every morning at 4 A.M. along with everyone on it. His uncles brought him food from the dining room and he was thankful to have made it.

Those two uncles—David and Rachmil Koschitski—left their families behind, thinking they would be able to send for them later.

"We thought that in war, it was the men who were in real danger," Rabbi Besser recalls. "Women and children were usually not harmed."

So David and Rachmil left their wives and twelve children in Poland.

The ship made its way across the Mediterranean, through the Greek Isles, past Cyprus, finally docking at 10 in the morning in Tel Aviv on September 5. Naftali and his wife were waiting at the pier, expecting only to see the uncles. Haskel had been unable to contact them before the ship left Constanta, so they had no idea that their son had safely escaped and was onboard. Seeing him was a miracle. Although they were overcome with relief, the celebration was somewhat muted because their daughter and her husband, along with so many others, were still in Poland.

The contrast between Europe and Palestine could not have been starker. In 1939, British-controlled Palestine was a relatively safe place for Jews. Within two weeks of his arrival in Tel Aviv, Germany had swallowed Poland. It quickly dawned on Haskel that he was living in a very different world from the one he had left.

"It's hard to describe; it's like going from one planet to another. Maybe it was even greater than that. We were free but our hearts were bleeding because of everything that was going on in Poland."

The enormity of what had just transpired started to sink in.

"I began to realize that I somehow—almost recklessly—escaped this inferno. And instead I came into a heaven. Palestine at that time was a real Garden of Eden. Every day I would walk several miles on the beach, walking, thinking. The sky was a beautiful blue and the sea was a comfort to me, especially after hearing all the news."

The Besser apartment on Gordon Street in Tel Aviv became a center—this time for Jews who left families in Europe. As in Katowice, there was a large dining-room table often serving thirty people on any given night. Again, everyone was welcome.

Naftali Besser had a keen understanding of the political situation earlier than most people and had transferred much of his wealth to Palestine. It wasn't easy, but there were ways in which this could be done. With the exception of rent, life was relatively inexpensive. Food was plentiful because agriculture, the chief industry created by the Zionists, could not be exported—there was virtually no transportation due to the war. Here there was a glut of produce when much of Europe was starving.

Haskel immediately became a local celebrity by starting a nightly war briefing. In his own methodical way, he reviewed the daily situation with maps and small flags and colored pins all compiled from shortwave radio reports—German, Russian, Swiss, and the BBC.

"I was an avid listener. Occasionally I could hear American radio, but it was harder to tune in."

The less formal Israeli style began to make its mark on this very European family.

"I still had my beard and sidelocks. But I began to take off my jacket and sometimes walk around in shirtsleeves. I even wore a straw hat, but not on Shabbos."

Palestine in 1939 was a fascinating mix of the ancient Middle East and modern Europe. There had been a Jewish presence in that area since Roman times. But the modern Zionist movement, which had begun over forty years earlier, was responsible not just for a rebirth, but a dramatic face-lift as well. The Zionists created Tel Aviv, a modern city on the sea. By 1939, the city was made up of two different styles of architecture. There was an Eastern European aesthetic developed through the 1920s, as the majority of Jews in the first wave emigrated from Poland and Russia. But the 1930s saw a large influx of German and Austrian Jews who brought modernism. Given the climate, this second style actually worked better. The modern designs offered more open space within the buildings, which in turn allowed more airflow, especially helpful during the stifling summers, long before the days of air-conditioning.

"The German influence made the city more beautiful," says the rabbi.

That German influence extended beyond the city's architecture. It seemed more people spoke German than Hebrew, and German and Austrian Jews brought café culture with them. Viennese coffee shops sprung up and most business was conducted in the outdoor cafés where people seemed to spend at least an hour or two every day. There were also the ladies who came every afternoon to have tea and cakes in their best dresses (often their only dresses)— one more effort to hold on to the old world and something familiar in what was otherwise a strange new land.

The German Jews also brought classical music, which could be heard everywhere. There were music societies, orchestras, and nightly concerts.

"People walked everywhere, there were no cars. You would greet people on the street. It was a very nice, relaxed life—very cultured."

That's why the Bessers were there. Most Hasidim lived in Jerusalem. The Bessers were among the relatively few religious Jews who lived in Tel Aviv. They enjoyed the cosmopolitan nature of the city but they traveled to Jerusalem for all of the important holidays.

"Tel Aviv was a living city," Rabbi Besser recalls. "Jerusalem was beautiful, but in those days it was an old-age home."

Of course, all of this was set against the backdrop of what was going on in Europe. The entire continent was in flames. And with communication almost impossible, families had no idea what was happening to their loved ones. For those who left family and friends behind in Europe—and that was practically everyone—anxiety was a constant.

Strangely, with the war really not that far away, Palestine was left untouched. It could have been different. Just to the north, Lebanon was a French colony. Even though it was not officially aligned with Vichy France, the French governor, General Dentz, was sympathetic to the Nazis and allowed German planes to land there. This put Palestine easily within range of the Luftwaffe. Yet, the only real danger to Palestine came in the autumn of 1940 when two Italian planes suddenly appeared over Tel Aviv and dropped several bombs on a residential area.

"I was home listening to the war news from Berlin, which came on every afternoon between two and four. I heard the bombs go off."

Haskel's uncles were near the beach at the time and saw the event from a different angle. They watched as the two planes flew very high in the air. The planes dropped their bombs and, just as quickly as they had come, they were gone. It was over almost before it began. In press reports the Italians claimed they bombed the refineries in Haifa. But that could not have been further from the truth.

"Those refineries in the port of Haifa were about sixty miles away. It's hard to make that kind of mistake. On the other hand, it is possible they didn't know what they had attacked.

"There were no military targets in Tel Aviv whatsoever. And because of that, there was no air defense. The planes could have flown over the rooftops and machine-gunned anyone they wanted. There was no one to protect us."

More than two hundred people were killed in the bombing. Most of the population became unhinged for about two weeks, but when nothing more followed, things returned to normal. Haskel witnessed a psychological phenomenon that was not uncommon in those years. The people of Tel Aviv got used to the possibility of sudden death, as people did in many cities around the world. The attitude seemed to be one of acceptance.

"People get killed . . . they get killed . . . life goes on: that seemed to be the general attitude," remembers the rabbi.

The Italians never came back. But the incident raised a different question in Haskel Besser's mind: Why didn't Hitler attempt to kill all the Jews in Palestine? There were, after all, 600,000 with no defenses whatsoever.

"After the war, we found out that one of Hitler's main goals was to annihilate the Jews. In 1944, he sacrificed Berlin by sending six Panzer divisions to occupy Hungary in order to kill all the Jews there, rather than try to stop the Russian advance into Prussia and save German women and children.

"Five German planes could have done the job," the rabbi says. "I believe it is one of the miracles of the war. It doesn't balance the numbers of those lost. But perhaps it demonstrates the sanctity of the Holy Land."

THE TORMENTED SOUL

Newspapers were delivered in an unusual fashion in Palestine. Because of the oppressive heat during the summer months, people left all of their windows open. Very early every morning, delivery boys would simply throw the paper through open windows from the street.

"This is how I was awakened every morning at four-thirty. It was a unique system. I would hear a *clunk* in the next room and knew it was time to get up. We actually had to move any glass objects away from the drop zone. With the *clunk*, I would get up, wash, and look at the paper."

The streets were always deserted at that hour. But one morning, when Haskel went to retrieve the paper, he looked out and thought he saw someone looking at him from the street.

"I didn't exactly see anyone, but I had the feeling and I wondered: 'Was someone there?'"

The next morning, when he went to get the paper, he did see someone. It was hard to identify the person in the shadows, but he saw that it was a Hasidic rabbi. This was unusual for Gordon Street, which was not a Hasidic neighborhood. When he looked again, the figure had vanished.

"The next day, I was looking to see if he was there again, but I didn't want to show myself because I was in my pajamas. This time I was able to get a good look and I recognized him. It was the son of the Gerer Rebbe."

After his father's death, when he became the Gerer Rebbe, this man would be one of the most important rebbes in the world—a giant in the Hasidic world. But even then, he had already developed a reputation as one of the leading scholars and teachers in the Jewish world.

"He was very stern and he didn't say a lot—he was not a talker—but when he spoke, he spoke with great force."

This man was tormented by the events in Europe, but could never discuss it in public. It wasn't just the mass destruction of the Jewish people and the loss of the Hasidic world that tortured him. The tragedy was personal. The future rebbe lost his beloved wife and his two children, a son and daughter. But, because of his position, he had no one to lean on. So he would walk . . . all night long. That's when he passed the Besser house.

Years after the war, and in the most reticent way, he permitted himself to ask someone about it. He was walking with Naftali Lavi—who later became Israel's counsel general in the United States and was a survivor of the camps. He turned to Lavi and asked: "You saw the smoke at Auschwitz?" and Lavi answered, "Yes." That was the extent of the conversation. The rebbe just stood still for ten minutes saying nothing—just thinking.

As far as anyone knows, he never talked about the Holocaust in public again.

"But it was on his mind all the time. Poland was the spring that gave life to Judaism, the grand dynasties of Hasidism in Poland were extinguished, destroyed. And everyone who remained from that world couldn't understand what happened and how to absorb this reality. Many believed the Jewish world would not continue as it had before."

The Bessers focused most of their energy on attempting to save Jews in Poland. To help, they used whatever legal means they had at their disposal. Many Polish Jews immediately sought citizenship in Palestine, which would make wives and children still in Poland British citizens as well. Then they hoped for an exchange of foreign nationals sometime down the road. They worked with lawyers. They worked with the Red Cross. They even tried to go through the Vatican. Three exchanges eventually took place, but they didn't all work out as the Bessers had hoped. One cousin could have come to Palestine in the first exchange set up through the Red Cross, but she became too sick to

travel and couldn't leave. Eventually she perished. In another case, David Koschitski's wife, Miriam, and her seven
children received exit papers, but she refused to go without her mother. She gave her exit visa to her sister-in-law,
Bronia, who had two children of her own. Bronia pleaded
with Miriam to at least let her take some of the children.
Miriam eventually relented and gave her two—the rest
would perish.

"It's just a big, tragic story," the rabbi says, looking back
on it.

An Amazing Courage

That sister-in-law who survived in Miriam's place, Bronia,
had been a true hero in Poland. Before the war, she had
lived in Germany for ten years and spoke fluent German.
After the Germans occupied Poland, she put her life in danger constantly and traveled between the Russian and German zones in order to bring Jews out, bring them food or
money, and help in any way she could.

Prior to the German invasion of Russia, the Russians
controlled part of Poland. The other part was occupied and
administered by the Germans. It was safer for Jews in the
Russian zone.

Bronia began traveling between the two zones without
any travel papers—a crime punishable by death. The
method she used showed amazing daring coupled with intelligence. Since high-ranking German officers always traveled in first class, she would look for the officer with the
highest rank and go into his compartment as a way to evade
the military police on the train.

"The officers were always very gallant and they liked pretty women," Rabbi Besser remembers. "She would immediately strike up a conversation in flawless German."

Women rarely traveled in those days. The trains were almost always filled with military personnel. So it was a pleasant break for the officer to have the company of a German-speaking woman on the trip.

"When the military police came to that compartment, the officer would always wave them off," said the rabbi. "He didn't want to be bothered and the MP didn't question the officer."

Once she arrived at her destination, she would arrange to have Jews smuggled out to the Russian zone by horse and cart. She would offer encouragement. Then she would travel back the same way. She was caught only once, and that is a story in itself.

One day, a conductor asked her for her papers. Since she had neither papers nor a ticket, he demanded to see her passport. The conductor was dumbfounded to see the large letter "J" stamped on it.

"You are a Jew?" he asked.

"Yes," she replied.

"Then why aren't you wearing an armband?" he asked.

She said nothing.

The conductor called for a military police officer, who took her off the train and down to police headquarters. She had been carrying a thermos bottle, which had nothing inside to drink. It was filled with money—another capital offense. The officer who came into the room to do the interrogation stared at her for a long time. Then he finally spoke.

"Are you a mother?" he asked.

"Yes," she responded in German.

"You'll be shot for this, you know," said the officer. "And then what will happen to your children?"

He stared at her again for a long time and then he spoke again.

"If I look the other way, maybe you'll escape," he suggested.

She wasn't sure what to do—was he just looking for a reason to shoot her or was he sincere? She had been studying him all this time and she felt he was offering her a real way out. He turned around and she left as quickly as she could. She was barely out of the office and into the hallway when she heard the man start to shout and her worst fears began to materialize. But he didn't want to shoot her. He was running after her because she left her thermos on his desk.

When she finally arrived at her home, much later than expected, everyone was upset. They didn't know what had happened to her and they feared the worst. Their fears had been compounded by the prophetic warning that came from the Radomsker Rebbe in Warsaw. The message: "Don't make this particular journey during this week."

ONLY DARKNESS

It was after one of the first exchanges of Jews in 1940 that the true extent of the horror began to be understood in Palestine.

"We knew the Germans were shooting Jews. But there's a difference between 'shooting ten Jews here, or even twenty' and liquidating city after city."

The horrible stories just continued to come with every person who managed to escape. More and more people—aunts, cousins, friends—were just gone. And then there was news that devastated Naftali. The Radomsker Rebbe—his spiritual leader and close friend—had been killed along with his entire family. It was a bleak time.

"I don't think my father was ever the same after he heard the news about the rebbe," says Rabbi Besser. "And I think it led to his own premature death.

"It was hard to believe that the world we grew up in, the world we knew, had suddenly expired. It vanished. Now I look back, I accept it. But at that time, it was hard to accept and impossible to understand. It was all beyond our grasp."

The number of dead grew so large that it was often impossible to comprehend the individual horror. Many years later, Rabbi Besser seems to deal with this phenomenon by talking about a very few individuals, like Israel Chaim.

Israel Chaim was a cousin who was three years younger than Haskel. Sixty years later, the rabbi still remembers him with such fondness.

"He was an unusually intelligent boy," Rabbi Besser recalls. "He was so quick and so pleasant."

Once when he came to visit the Bessers in Poland, the young cousin, who was then around ten, excitedly announced that he had met Haskel's colleh (his future bride). Haskel was only thirteen at the time and was interested since he was pretty sure he was not engaged.

"Oh," he replied. "Who is she?"

"Every girl I've seen would like to be your colleh," Israel answered with a smile.

Within a year of his bar mitzvah, Israel Chaim was dead at the hands of the Nazis. Rabbi Besser has grown into manhood, had a family, and lived an extraordinary life. But to the rabbi and those few people who still might remember him, Israel Chaim is forever a boy.

Sixty years later, Rabbi Besser still misses him.

FIVE

I HAD NO CHOICE

While Tel Aviv was the most modern city in Palestine, Jerusalem was the most sacred. For this reason, Haskel and Naftali made the two-hour trip to Jerusalem for every Jewish holiday. However, in October 1940 Naftali was not able to join Haskel for the celebration of Simchas Torah.

It was shortly after the Italian bombing of Tel Aviv and both cities were blacked out at night. After sunset on the night that the holiday began, Haskel was having a hard time making his way back from the Western Wall to his hotel in the pitch dark. Suddenly, as he turned a corner, he found himself swept up by a wave of Orthodox Jews who were singing and dancing through the streets. These men swept him up and pulled him along into their group.

"I had no choice," he jokes. "They took me by force."

Actually, they were supposed to bring any Jews they came across and Haskel was obliged to go. The holiday of Simchas Torah celebrates the completion of the reading of the Torah. It takes exactly one year to read the entire Torah and on this holiday, which always falls in autumn, twelve days after Yom Kippur, the final chapter of the Torah is read, followed immediately by the very beginning (literally "the beginning": the Torah begins with the first line of Genesis). This way, by reading the end and the beginning together, there is never a break.

It is considered a great honor to be chosen by one's synagogue to read one of these two passages. These men are called the chasan Torah and the chasan Breishis, the *groom* of the Torah and the *prince* of the Torah.

The men who dragged Haskel along were going to the home of a chasan Breishis where he was celebrating this honor with an open house. The home was overcrowded and stifling. The host, Beryl Ludmir, immediately noticed that Haskel was a stranger and European because he wore a tie—unusual for Israel. Beryl asked him where he was from and they had a short conversation. Both Beryl and his wife were seventh-generation Jerusalemites and the descendants of some of the most famous rabbis in history.

His wife, Hasia Rifka, was the great-granddaughter of Rabbi Joseph Schlesinger, a passionate Zionist who left Bratislava in 1870 at the age of twenty-two. Traveling to Palestine in that period, three decades before the birth of modern Zionism, was not easy. But Schlesinger made the trip several times, to help start the movement of bringing Jews back to the Holy Land.

Beryl was directly descended from the first Lubavitcher Rebbe, Shneur Zalman, who died in 1812 under the czar's protection. It was unusual for a Russian czar to look after a Hasidic rebbe, but Czar Alexander I did this because Zalman sided with him in his war against Napoleon. (That in itself was unusual because Napoleon was more inclined to help Jews than any czar. Zalman took the czar's side not be-cause he liked him, but because he realized that although Jews would be better off physically under Napoleon, he thought they would become less observant in a more liberal culture that was more open to assimilation.)

Rabbi Besser still chuckles remembering how, in that stifling house, Beryl insisted that he have some of the kugel (noodle pudding) that was on the table—something that did not look very appealing to him.

Haskel found Beryl Ludmir to be a very warm man who went out of his way to make sure Haskel felt welcome. That was that. He didn't think much more about the brief meeting.

But a few weeks later, Haskel was in Jerusalem again, with a friend. The man suggested that they have coffee with an acquaintance and, to his surprise, he found himself in front of that same house.

"I know this place," Haskel said. "I was just here re-cently."

Haskel was an exceptionally bright young man, but he still didn't pick up on the fact that this may have been more than just coincidence.

Again he met Beryl, but this time, as the three men were talking in the parlor, a young woman came in.

"This is my daughter," said Beryl. "She's my right hand. She keeps my books. She watches over all of my business."

Later, Haskel would learn that this wasn't quite true.

"I think he had a plan—he wanted to improve her ré-sumé, but it wasn't necessary."

Haskel was only seventeen. From the time he was fif-teen, various people in Poland had suggested to his parents that he might be a good "chusen" for various young women. But because of the situation leading up to their escape, his father and he had agreed it was not the time.

If seventeen seems young, it is not in Orthodox circles. Marriages can be arranged even earlier, although the actual wedding doesn't take place until the couple is in their late teens. The Talmud suggests eighteen as the right age for marriage, but it still depends on other factors: the maturity of the couple and whether there is an older sibling who is not yet married. A boy or girl will hold off a marriage until older brothers or sisters have gone to their chupah (the canopy under which all Jewish weddings take place).

Haskel already had one offer. There was a very wealthy man who was eager for Haskel to marry his daughter. Although the young woman liked Haskel, she didn't care for his Orthodox garb. In fact, she was specific—she didn't want Haskel to wear a streimel on all holidays as well as Shabbos. The girl's family was religious, but not Hasidic.

The girl's father got wind of the problem and made Haskel a secret proposal: if he agreed to marry his daughter and postponed wearing a streimel and if four months after the wedding the bride still insisted that he not wear it, his prospective father-in-law would pay him 100,000 pounds. Today, that would be worth well over $1 million.

Later, Haskel found out just what a brilliant mind this man had for business. The man also had two sons and one of those sons was interested in Beryl Ludmir's daughter. If Haskel were to marry this man's daughter, his prospective father-in-law would, effectively, take care of two concerns at once.

It didn't matter though; Haskel's streimel was not for sale. But the decision was not solely his. A little over a year after meeting Beryl Ludmir, during Chanukah 1941, Haskel accompanied his father to the shul of Israel's most famous rabbi at the time, Israel Friedman, the Husiatiner Rebbe.

The custom for this visit was to give the rabbi a kvitol and a pidion. The pidion was a donation, for the rabbi's synagogue. The kvitol was a small piece of paper that included Naftali's name along with the names of his wife, his children, and a description of any problems he may be facing.

The rebbe focused on Haskel and asked how old he was. He then asked Naftali if he had considered any collehs for his son. Naftali responded that there was an offer and mentioned the name of the wealthy family. The Husiatiner Rebbe seemed to ignore what Naftali just told him and instead asked if he had thought about Beryl Ludmir's daughter.

"Well, yes," Naftali told the rebbe. He had met Beryl Ludmir, but wondered if there might be too much of a gulf between the two families since Ludmir was a sabra (native born) and the Bessers were European.

"I think Beryl Ludmir's daughter would be good," the Husiatiner Rebbe replied, short and to the point.

Once outside, Naftali turned to his son.

"Did you hear the rebbe?" he asked. "It seems perfectly clear. It will be Beryl Ludmir's daughter." In Naftali's mind, that was that.

But it wasn't perfectly clear to Haskel and that wasn't his interpretation of the conversation. As a teenager, Haskel did not yet have the rock-solid belief in a rebbe's suggestions that Naftali had. That would come in time. But Haskel didn't question his father's understanding of the rebbe's suggestion. If he had any reservations, he never voiced them.

Before Naftali agreed to the marriage, he wanted to get to know the Ludmir family a little better. So he traveled to Jerusalem by himself to spend a Shabbos with them. Upon his return, he seemed even more in favor of the union.

The very next day, Haskel traveled back to Jerusalem to formally meet the young woman, Liba Ludmir. The two teenagers spent about an hour and a half talking to each other. These ninety minutes would have a profound impact on their lives.

Sixty years later and with the insight of age, the rabbi tries to explain just what transpired in that room between these two seventeen-year-olds that made them feel they could make such a momentous decision.

"My father and the rebbe seemed to agree that this would be the right match. Of course, there had to be an attraction, and there was. In the end, it was still our decision."

Haskel and Liba simply sat in a room and talked. No dinner out, no movie, not even a stroll in the park. After all this time, the fact that some of the details of that meeting are still so clear is telling.

"I remember the color of her pullover. It was yellow. And I felt relieved when I realized that she was a very pretty girl," he remembers with a smile. "Whatever we discussed we were more or less on the same wavelength, except I noticed she was—politically—more to the right than I was. But that didn't bother me."

On reflection, Rabbi Besser is quite candid about where he stood at this juncture in his life.

"I knew the road of history and the details of many battles, I knew the Torah, I understood a great deal about music. But at this stage of life I had no experience with women whatsoever."

When he arrived back home in Tel Aviv, Haskel's mother was interested in his visit and coaxed him for details. Although Naftali was in the room, he said nothing.

What may seem astounding in this day and age is the outcome of this one visit: in that short time, Haskel Besser

knew that he wanted to marry Liba. Facing the huge adjust-
ment and compromises of marriage, Haskel agreed to the
shiduch (match) without hesitation.

Today, Rabbi Besser feels just as strongly that long en-
gagements are unnecessary. He thinks that the popular
trend of couples living together before they are married—
unheard of in his world—is a mistake. Divorce statistics actually back him up.

Although there had been an agreement to meet for a
second time, their next visit would be an engagement party,
which was all well and good—except that no one told Liba.
All she knew was that she was going to have another date
with this very intelligent and courtly young man with European manners and a warm sense of humor.

When Liba came into her home the following Monday,
she noticed that there was unusual activity in the house and,
even stranger, she smelled fish cooking in the kitchen. Since
fish is only cooked for Fridays and holidays and this was an
ordinary Monday, she asked what was going on. That's when
she found out that the meeting wasn't another date at all,
but her engagement party.

"Maybe she remembers that it was not with her explicit
approval," the rabbi recalls with a smile, "but now, so many
years later, she doesn't seem to mind."

Clearly, Liba did not object. Although she will never
talk about that meeting (or anything else of a personal nature with anyone outside her family), the fact is that she
could have said no. She did not.

All of this happened in January 1942. The wedding was
planned for that May.

During that time, Liba sent Haskel letters from her
home in Jerusalem to his home in Tel Aviv almost every
day (there was no long-distance telephone service readily

available in those days). The notes came on blue stationery. The marriage may have been arranged, the decision quick, but there was clearly a bond that was building between this young man and woman.

"Every day, I waited for the postman, looking for those blue letters," he remembers today. "I still have them."

As the wedding date drew near and everything appeared to be moving in the right direction, something happened that would subvert the plan. One Sunday, Haskel came home not feeling well. He lay down, but began to feel worse. When Naftali arrived home he was shocked to see Haskel looking so sickly and called the doctor. After a quick examination, an ambulance was called. In that short time, he could no longer walk and had to be carried downstairs and taken directly to the hospital. Haskel had contracted both encephalitis and meningitis, probably from a mosquito. His headaches were so painful that the slightest noise caused excruciating pain. Anyone who entered his room had to remove their shoes because the slightest step was agony for him.

Germany's racial laws had resulted in a windfall of medical talent in Tel Aviv. Some of the finest doctors in the world were now living there. In fact, the main language spoken in hospitals at that time was German. One day, when a nurse asked the doctor about the case, they inadvertently gave out more information than they should have.

"They did not know that I spoke German and they didn't know that I was conscious because my head was wrapped in bandages—I looked like a mummy."

The doctor gave a very gloomy prognosis: he thought Haskel would live, but the damage was probably permanent. He would perhaps be unable to walk and he might be crazy.

"I heard my future and I understood it."

This obviously should have been a dilemma for his new fiancée. Some friends of the Ludmir family suggested that they call off the engagement. They told Beryl that his future son-in-law would be an invalid and, for the sake of his daughter, he should cancel it. But neither Beryl nor Liba ever considered such a thought.

"I wouldn't have blamed them if they had left." But their actions made him realize that the fondness his future wife had for him was shared by his future father-in-law.

"I think they both loved me very much," he says. "The one person who kept me alive was my fiancée. She came every day and stayed morning till night. She gave me the moral and spiritual strength that I needed. And this cemented the strong relationship between us."

It also created a bond between Naftali and his future daughter-in-law. They traveled to the hospital together every day. He was impressed with her loyalty toward his son as well as her determination.

Very slowly, Haskel began to feel better. When the bandages were first removed from his head, he didn't just have double vision, he saw an object sixty-four times in a swirling kaleidoscope. Slowly that was halved to thirty-two times, then sixteen, and eventually he saw things as they were, although he would always need thick glasses after the illness. Even more upsetting, he had to relearn how to walk. He still remembers the fear in that first step.

"My father took one arm and my doctor took the other arm. It was perhaps the most difficult step of my life. I had no balance—I couldn't even hold my head up straight without having it flop down."

After several weeks in the hospital, Haskel was well enough to be transferred to a rest home. He was lucky since the only permanent damage besides the weakened eyesight was the loss of his hair. But he was still very weak and the rebbe was consulted to see if the wedding should continue as planned. The answer was yes.

A new date was set, the end of July, and the wedding process started up again. But then, yet another stumbling block arose, this time from the outside world and the cataclysmic turmoil that had until now spared this young couple.

THE DESERT FOX

A month before the wedding, in June 1942, Tobruk fell. Rommel's Panzer Corps suddenly broke through the British lines and drove on to Cairo.

"I knew there were no defenses left," Rabbi Besser, who had been closely watching the advance, remembers. "At El Alamein the Germans were about sixty miles from Alexandria, where the British Mediterranean Fleet was docked— and just fifty miles from the Suez Canal. Rommel was going thirty to forty miles a day. At that rate, he could be at the canal in forty-eight hours and after that, Palestine."

Jews realized the seriousness of the situation and felt helpless. They knew there was no army to protect them and they had a very clear idea of what to expect if the Germans came. Families like the Bessers who had escaped the Holocaust that was raging in Europe no longer felt safe. The murdering army had followed them to the Promised Land and now it truly seemed to be all over.

"All of Palestine was in a panic because we heard about the way the Germans were behaving. This time, there seemed to be no way out."

Various proclamations were posted on the street. The Haganah (the Jewish defense force that would later become the modern-day Israeli army) tried to reassure the population that it would protect them. The more extreme Irgun was less subtle, suggesting that everyone carry a knife and "take at least one German with them."

There was even a run on poison. Rabbi Besser recalls his next-door neighbor from Germany who told him he had three servings of cyanide: one for the himself, one his wife, and one for their little dog, Fifi.

Haskel witnessed something even more upsetting.

"The streets were filled with Arabs who were actually fighting among themselves over who was going to get which house. They said things like: 'I saw this house first, it's going to be mine.'"

Haskel and Liba did not know what would happen and, two weeks before the wedding, they secretly went off to have their photos taken.

"We didn't know if we'd be alive next week or where we'd be, so we thought, at least we'd have a picture of each other in case we were separated."

In the middle of all this chaos, Haskel's future father-in-law came to Tel Aviv to make plans for the wedding. People thought he was crazy. But Beryl Ludmir understood the gravity of the situation. Before he signed the contract with the hotel for the wedding reception, he went to the Husiatiner Rebbe (the same rebbe Naftali had seen on Chanukah) to ask his advice. This was on a Sunday. The rebbe said he would have an answer for him in a day or two.

In the Hasidic world, the Husiatiner Rebbe is considered one of the great prophets of the twentieth century. He left Austria in 1936, two years before the Anschluss. He

immigrated to Palestine and said openly that every Jew in
Europe should do the same. Unlike most of the Hasidic
rebbes, the Husiatiner saw it coming.

There was a reason the rebbe told Beryl to wait a few
days. It is customary to visit the graves of great rabbis and
sages on their yahrtzeit—the anniversary of their death. And
that Tuesday was the yahrtzeit of one of the greatest rabbis
in history, Chaim ben Eter, also known as the Ohr Hachaim
(the light of life). Ben Eter lived during the eighteenth century and was renowned for perhaps the most brilliant commentary on the Bible—one that is studied to this day. He is
buried in Har Hazeitim, the Mount of Olives, the famous
cemetery in Jerusalem.

So, with Rommel poised at Palestine's doorstep and no
conceivable protection for the population, thousands of religious Jews turned to the only power they knew. They
turned to G-d and fervent prayer—one that seemed to come
from their souls.

A fast day on the yahrtzeit was declared by the rebbes.
Upwards of twenty thousand people went to pray at this
man's grave. Beryl Ludmir accompanied the Husiatiner
Rebbe to the grave, and while the rebbe prayed, Beryl noticed that he seemed to fix his eyes on the words chiseled on
the gravestone.

After a long while, the rebbe turned to Beryl and said
simply: "It will be good. Make the wedding."

No one understood why the rebbe said this. But afterward Beryl went directly to the hotel and signed the con-
tract for the celebration.

Much later, Rabbi Besser went to the grave to try to figure out how the rebbe came to his conclusion.

"I saw nothing special," the rabbi recalls. But the
rebbe told Beryl that he had seen the Hebrew name of

God written in gold letters, floating in the air, above the gravestone. And he saw it written in the correct way—with all four letters in a row. "For him, this was the sign."

The yahrtzeit in 1942 began an amazing confluence of events that would change more than just Haskel and Liba's lives. The rebbe had not based his decision solely on what he saw over that grave. He had seen something else. While studying for that week's Torah parsha, the rebbe interpreted a commentary written hundreds of years before that he claimed (correctly, it turns out) freed the Jews from their death sentence.

The commentary was written by the Ohr Hachaim in the eighteenth century on the Torah parsha, Numbers 24:17. He interpreted the following story: In the Bible Jacob is called by two names, Jacob and Israel. When he is referred to as Jacob, things don't work very well for the people of Israel. But after he wrestles with the angel and he becomes known by his new name, Israel, the nation prospers. In the commentary, it says that if he is called Jacob, he will be killed by Rommel. The name Rommel was actually spelled out in Hebrew—almost two hundred years before the war. The commentary goes on to say that if Jacob is called Israel, Rommel will not destroy him and the nation will prevail.

It is more probable that the reference is to Romulus, one of the founders of Rome. But seeing the name Rommel spelled out phonetically, along with the lettering over the grave, was enough of a sign for the rebbe to declare that the Jews of Palestine would not be harmed.

At that moment, Field Marshal Erwin Rommel had advanced to the point that there were practically no British defenses in front of him. Had he continued, there would be nothing to stop him from capturing Palestine and then possibly Syria, Iraq, and Iran. With the capture of Iran, the entire underbelly of the Soviet Union would have been open to attack and the Russians would have had to divert troops to protect that border.

But that week, a huge sandstorm blew up out of the desert. It was impossible to go forward in those conditions. Rommel planned a tactical redeployment to a point where his tanks would be protected by hills. But Hitler had given his commanders strict orders that no German soldiers could retreat without his personal approval. Rommel sent Hitler a cable explaining his situation. Hitler cabled back saying absolutely not, no retreat.

Rommel sent another telegram trying to explain that this was not a retreat, it was only a temporary redeployment because of conditions. But Hitler would not okay it. Angry and frustrated, Rommel actually got on an airplane and flew back to Germany to see Hitler and explain the situation in person. Of course, it was not an easy trip. Rommel had to fly first to Tripoli, then to Sicily, and then on to Germany. The trip took close to twenty-four hours.

When he arrived at Hitler's headquarters, he was kept waiting for another eight hours.

When Hitler finally saw Rommel, he asked why he had come. Again Rommel explained his request for the redeployment of his troops. One more time, Hitler, now agitated, said there would be no retreats. One more time Rommel tried to make his point that this was not a retreat but a redeployment to service the tanks and give them new tracks, which were badly needed.

Finally Hitler understood and he gave Rommel the green light. But the trip wasted three days and proved to be the undoing of the Germans' African campaign.

When the Germans were ready for their next attack, they lost that month's full moon (attacks in the desert were made at night). So Rommel was forced to wait for the next month's full moon. The following month the weather did not cooperate. July is normally clear, but that year it rained and the skies were cloudy. So the attack was put off for another month. By this time, Churchill had placed a new commander in charge, Montgomery. It was Montgomery who stopped Rommel and his Afrika Korps in its tracks. The Germans never came any closer to Palestine.

After the war, Field Marshal Keitel, the commander of the German Army, wrote that June 30, 1942, was the moment Germany reached its zenith. After that point it was all downhill. From that day forward, the Germans continuously gave up ground until Berlin was conquered and the Third Reich lay in ruins.

June 30, 1942, was the same day that Beryl Ludmir stood with the Husiatiner Rebbe when he saw the name of G-d over the Ohr Hachaim's headstone.

The Jewish population settled down, life slowly went back to normal, and the Besser and Ludmir families planned their celebration.

THE CHUPAH

One of the things that Rabbi Besser remembers most clearly about his wedding is what wasn't. There was no music. And there were no photographs. Certain sects of Orthodox Jews did not permit them in Jerusalem because that is where the Temple was destroyed and, officially, all Jews are still in a state of mourning, even two thousand years later. His future father-in-law, Beryl, did not adhere to this rigid doctrine, but he did not want to offend those who did.

"They were very strict and there were no compromises."

Haskel Besser chose to break two rules, though. Collehs and chusens (brides and grooms) are supposed to fast on the day of their wedding. But because he had been so sick, Haskel was ordered by his doctors not to fast. In fact, the Husiatiner Rebbe sent a personal emissary to Haskel on the morning of the wedding with direct orders. The man brought a piece of cake from the rebbe and was told not to return until he personally watched Haskel eat it.

A bride and groom are also not supposed to see each other for at least a week before the ceremony. The couple held to that rule for the entire seven days before. But right before the event, Haskel wanted to see Liba, so he found out the time she would be going to the Western Wall before the ceremony. It was customary for brides and grooms in Jerusalem to visit the Wall before their wedding to place prayers in the cracks. It was 11 A.M., three hours before the ceremony.

Haskel made sure he would be there at that time. He met his bride just before noon on the day of their wedding and they exchanged a few words.

The chief rabbi, who conducted the wedding ceremony, was known as the Presburger Rebbe. But there were actually eight rabbis there, one more than necessary to perform each of the seven traditional blessings. Among them was Liba's uncle, who was one of the leaders of the two rabbinates of Jerusalem.

Liba's grandfather also took part, as did the head of Agudah Israel, Rabbi Yitzak Mayer Lewin. (Agudah is an Orthodox political organization that would later play a major role in Haskel Besser's life.)

Because the wedding was on a Friday afternoon, the event was incorporated into Shabbos. There were about three hundred people at the chupah, which was in the Hotel Babad. There was a small reception afterward, with cake and drinks. Then, with Shabbos approaching, everyone began to prepare.

Nothing is more sacred in the Jewish calendar than Shabbos. The age-old ritual of going to the mikvah, or ritual bath, was conducted, followed by Friday night prayers. But on this Shabbos over five hundred guests came together for a dinner that went far into the night. Haskel and Liba could not retire to their room until well after midnight.

"I remember it was terribly hot and there were a lot of mosquitoes, so it was difficult to sleep. Then just as I was about to settle down, people outside began to shout."

Two more very important rabbis—the Lelower Rebbe, Rabbi Moishe Mordechai Biderman, and Rabbi Shzuri who was the director general of the chief rabbinate (Rabbi Isaac Herzog)—had walked a great distance and weren't able to get there earlier. Since their presence was a great honor, Haskel came down again and didn't retire until after 2 A.M.

Because it was Shabbos, the group did what was normally done. They discussed the Torah parsha for that week and sang hymns. The next day, after the Shabbos service, there was a lunch for seven hundred people, and in the evening another huge dinner at 6:30 called the seudah shlishis (the traditional meal just before the Sabbath comes to an end). After Shabbos came to its official end at sundown on Saturday, music was allowed, although only a drum and castanets. This party also went on until about 2 A.M.

And it didn't stop there.

The festivities continued for a week. Every night for seven nights, Haskel and Liba were the guests of honor at cel-

ebrations known as the sheva brochas. Rather than go away
alone on a honeymoon, an Orthodox bride and groom celebrate with friends and relatives every night for seven days.

Shortly after this hectic wedding week, Haskel got sick
again. This time it was pneumonia and he was sick for several weeks. The two illnesses were the bookends of his wedding. For the first three years of their marriage, Haskel and
Liba lived with his parents. "My wife loved it," he remembers. A close friendship had developed between Liba and
Naftali during Haskel's illnesses. Naftali and Beryl had also
grown quite close.

After he recovered, Haskel continued his nightly war
updates for the local community. The house continued to
be a place where people would congregate, especially those
with relatives still in Europe. And they continued their efforts to get Jews out of Europe.

But his life had changed: Haskel was now a married
man.

Six

WE'RE STILL TOO CLOSE

After more than half a century and a revolution in technology, it's hard to comprehend how much more difficult it was in 1945 to get a message to someone far away. Long-distance phone lines were extremely limited and very expensive. The two most common methods of correspondence were letters and telegrams. Letters took weeks or even months to arrive and, since many ships were sunk during the war, many letters went down with them. Telegrams were more rapid but too expensive for regular use, and they were most often used for sending bad news. In America, the sight of a telegram delivery boy on a bicycle coming down the street during the war shot panic through the hearts of everyone who saw him coming since this was the method the War Department often used to inform families of casualties.

Throughout the spring of 1945, telegram after telegram began arriving in the Besser home for friends, acquaintances, and themselves. Each one carried heartbreak.

The immediate Besser family was intact, but most Jewish families in Palestine were not as lucky. (Haskel's sister and her husband, Mordechai, eventually made their way to Palestine, in a long, complicated journey that took them from Krakow to Trieste to Rome to Tangiers—where they spent a year—to Lisbon to Tanganyika to Kenya to Sudan to Cairo to Alexandria and finally to Tiberias. All of this was accomplished with a great deal of money sent by the family along with travel documents purchased in Tel Aviv.)

The two uncles who had traveled on the boat with Haskel back in 1939 had lived out the entire war in Palestine, not knowing the fate of their families. David Koschitski had a wife and seven children still there. Rachmil Koschitski left his wife, Beila, in Poland with five children. In April, just weeks before the surrender, Rachmil received a telegram from Germany, which stated simply: "Mother died. I'm here with Bronia Koschitski [a cousin] and two of David's children." It was signed by his daughter, Chaia. When Rachmil learned that his wife had died, perhaps along with some of his children, it was assumed that he would sit shiva for her, but he refused.

"Not yet," he said. He wanted more confirmation.

Months later, after his daughter arrived in Palestine and she related the circumstances of her mother's death, a strange telegram arrived from someone claiming to be Beila. It said she was alive and in a hospital.

Both Chaia and a doctor who had been with her when her mother died said that was impossible. It couldn't be her. It was probably someone who found her papers and was trying to get to Palestine. They had both seen her dead. During a forced march near the end of the war, they had to leave her by the side of the road in the snow. She had been delirious with a high fever. They didn't even have time to bury her. The SS guards ordered them to just leave her there in the snow and keep moving.

No, they said sadly, it was probably an impostor.

Beila had indeed been left at the side of the road. But shortly after the Jewish prisoners were pushed on by the guards, British soldiers arrived. The British found her and nursed her back to life. It was Beila Koschitski who had sent the telegram and she would be reunited with her family and live for another twenty-five years.

David was not as lucky as his brother, Rachmil. His wife and five of his seven children perished. The two who survived were brought out by their aunt during that earlier exchange. (It had been David's wife who would not leave without her mother.)

It was a very bleak time. Jews had an inverse reaction to the rest of the world as the war moved into its final, triumphant phase. Germany crumbled and victory was in sight. But as the mighty Allied armies crushed Hitler's fortress from all directions, the vast scope of the horror came into focus. When the war in Europe finally ended in May 1945, there was relief, of course. But there were no wild celebrations in Tel Aviv like the ones in Trafalgar and Times Square. In fact, although Rabbi Besser remembers the date, he has no real recollection of what he did that day.

"What I remember more were the telegrams from so many relatives in Europe," he says looking back on it. "When the atom bomb was dropped and the war finally ended, I was happy. I felt no remorse about it. That may sound harsh, but this was not a war like other wars. This was a war between good and evil. If Germany and Japan had been victorious, I am convinced there would be no world today. It would have been a world of Sodom and Gomorrah because Germany was so evil—every aspect. They murdered and tortured so many millions of people for nothing."

The rabbi also grapples with the question of why—why did the Germans do what they did?

"They had no conflict with the Jews. The Germans fought the French. They had done that before. They fought with Russia. We understood that. They fought Poland, England. We can comprehend the reasons countries go to war against other countries. But there is no rational explanation why they focused all of their hatred on us.

"They had no fight with the Jews. The Jewish population of Germany was so unimportant and many Jews were actually quite loyal to the Fatherland. Why they hated us so much, I still don't understand."

This question has vexed humanity for over half a century. After a flood of scholarly books, debates, government decrees, museums, movies, even Holocaust deniers and wars that were waged in response to the world's lack of response back then, mankind has had time to consider this question and digest it. So, too, has the rabbi.

One day, in the middle of a discussion on the Holocaust, he said something surprising.

"Believe me," he said, "I wanted to survive. I'm not a masochist who likes problems. I felt lucky to be out of the Holocaust. But I feel that I also missed being included in the mass of suffering."

This was a very unusual statement for someone who had just barely escaped the inferno, but the rabbi dismissed the notion of survivor's guilt. "Modern psychiatric methods," he calls it as he waves it off. "They are always trying to put a mantle on everything."

No, he didn't feel any guilt. He actually felt envy. He envied the people who were able to demonstrate such humanity in the face of such indescribable horror. Even more, he admired the people who were able to show their continued devotion to G-d. He explains this with a story from one of the ghettos. In the midst of the terrible suffering and hunger and stench, a father and son continued their study of Torah every day without fail. One day, SS soldiers came in and made another selection, choosing a few more to go to the gas chambers.

"'You, you, and you . . . out,' the soldiers ordered them," the rabbi tells the story. "And this time, the father was included in the group that would leave for the train. He said good-bye to his son, touched his face, and started walking with the others. But before he was out of sight, he turned and called out to the boy: 'Remember, we're on page seventy-four.'

"You see it's our duty to continue to learn, no matter what. There were some people who were famous professors or rabbis and, unfortunately, in those dehumanizing situations, they would steal a piece of bread from another inmate. On the other hand, there were people who were not known as great people, maybe they weren't educated, but they showed they had a princely nature."

In the ongoing debate over the past fifty years G-d is never far from the discussion. Clearly, asserts one point of view, if the Holocaust shows us anything, it shows us that there is no G-d. And even if you can begin to comprehend the slaughter of adults, which is nearly impossible, how do you deal with the wholesale butchery of one and a half million children? The question asked over and over is, Why did G-d abandon his people?

The rabbi's view falls on the opposite side of the equation.

"What happened to the Jews is more proof that there *is* a G-d and we are His people. And we are different from other people, because, otherwise, it's implicit that we were picked for nothing."

The ones who prove that G-d did not abandon his people, in the rabbi's mind, were not so much the partisans or those who fought the Nazis wherever they could (although he has great admiration for them). They are, instead, people like the father who reminded his son to continue to study as he left him for the gas chamber. Or the group of men who shared the tefillin they secretly hid in their barracks. They would lose the precious little sleep they were allowed to get up early and take turns putting them on each morning in order to daven. These are the people he has thought about and these are the people he has been more and more impressed with over the years.

"I'm curious if I would have passed the test. I wouldn't want to have failed it. And, of course, I always asked, Why me? Why did I escape? Why was I picked out? Why?"

In his own way, Rabbi Besser has spent the past sixty years trying to undo the inhumanity of that time by displaying an even greater humanity. It's almost as if he were trying single-handedly to chip away a wall of cruelty to somehow right a great wrong. Whether it's handing money to any outstretched hand, or giving his time to anyone who asks, or simply being courteous on the street, his gentlemanly behavior has a purpose. There is, of course, one more piece to this mosaic. He has also spent his life trying to help rebuild what was left of his people.

"In the five-thousand-year history of the Jews, this is the single worst event to befall us," he once remarked. "There were two distinct worlds—the world before and the world after. And there might as well have been a ten-thousand-year gulf between the two because they are so completely different. That old world was my world. It was an amazing and beautiful world of three and a half million Polish Jews, along with extraordinary and wonderful rebbes and tens of thousands of devoted yeshiva students. I was there. I know what it looked like and how it was. I can still see it and smell it and almost touch it."

The rabbi understands he is a living witness to an extinct world. And it's a world that he often misses. True, he's always been very much a part of the present. He's loved New York since the day he arrived. He loves to be in Israel. But it's that old world—the world of his fathers—for which he feels a deeper affinity.

Sixty years doesn't seem to be enough for the world to comprehend the enormity of the Second World War. The scope of it all is still impossible for the human mind to imagine. In this regard, Rabbi Besser is no different from anyone else. But unlike many, he has also struggled with a different, more personal issue over the decades: the greatest crime in the history of the Jews was committed by the people he most revered.

"I had such admiration for that country. Germany was a Golden Land. I loved everything that was there . . . its culture, its science, its competence. And then suddenly, immediately, Germany changed into an evil never seen before in the civilized world.

"If this happened to the Jews in Poland or Russia, I might be able to understand. In Hungary, fifty percent of the doctors and lawyers were Jews. But in Germany, the percentage of the population that was Jewish was minute—less than one percent.

"Yes, there were certain businesses where the Jews made themselves felt—medicine, retail stores, literature—but the great industries of Germany were controlled by non-Jews. There's no logical reason for what the Germans did.

This was not done by a wild, primitive people. It was done by cultured people, university graduates who were not drunk on vodka and in the mood to kill.

"Industrialists, generals, and bureaucrats sat down without excitement and made a plan: How many liters of gas could kill so many children. They used slide rules to calculate this equation."

So what was it? How did this cultured, advanced country take the sudden and frightening turn into barbarism? There have been so many reasons that people have come up with to help explain how the country of Beethoven and Brahms could produce Auschwitz and Treblinka and Babi Yar. The rabbi has heard them all, from economic theories to the mesmerizing effect that Hitler had on crowds—something he knows firsthand. Ultimately, for the rabbi, none of the explanations really answers the question.

Rabbi Besser has concluded, after a great deal of thought, that the reason Hitler wanted to destroy the Jews comes down to religion. Not what Jews did or what they controlled or how they looked. It was their religion.

"Hitler was not a religious man. I never heard him use the word *G-d*. He used the word *Vorsehung*—a great power, but somewhere between G-d and man: one who has the power to foresee. When I listened on the radio to Hitler's speeches, his voice would rise as a warning to Jews. He would say Vorsehung will save us from this affliction—the affliction he was talking about, of course, was the Jews.

"He believed in something, though. He believed that the white race, Aryans in particular, was destined to lead the world. Whether this was accomplished by G-d or nature he didn't say."

In order to prove that the Germans were the master race, Hitler had to show that Jews, who were often referred to as the chosen people, were not chosen at all. But in Rabbi Besser's mind, it is important to understand the correct definition of chosen people.

"When we say we are the chosen people, we *never* say we were chosen to rule the world. We were chosen only to learn the Torah. That is all. We're happy for that, but it's not an easy life. We must pray several times every day. We are not allowed to eat all the good food. We must always be studying. It's not easy."

Obviously, there is a huge distinction between the German concept of racial superiority and the way the Jews perceive themselves.

"We have an open door. Anyone can become Jewish. All you have to do is want to be Jewish and study. But the Germans said 'No, in order to be considered an Aryan, you must be an Aryan for so many generations. You must have certain qualifications: such eyes, such a nose, even the correct ears.' It was a very exclusive club."

"Because we are the chosen people, we are chosen for good *and* bad. Here it was for bad. We were chosen for that. When you think about it, it's the only explanation. If you are not religious, then you have no other explanation. It doesn't make sense."

Since the Jews posed no geopolitical threat to the Germans, the rabbi believes that Hitler gambled and sacrificed the German people for his conviction that the Aryans, not the Jews, were the chosen people.

He offers a military example: in May 1944, the Russians, still outside the German border, started a huge double offensive, which threatened to penetrate into Prussia for the first time. Hitler still held six tank divisions in reserve near the Swiss border. He called in Field Marshal Keitel and told him to mobilize the six Panzer divisions. Keitel told him that he had anticipated the order and had put them on alert three hours earlier. He told Hitler he could have them in position the next day to meet the Russians. To Keitel's astonishment, Hitler told him he didn't want those units in Prussia. Instead, he wanted them sent to Hungary.

When Keitel reminded his leader that wasn't where the Soviets were attacking and, besides, Hungary was an ally, Hitler coldly dismissed him, declaring abruptly, "That is my order." Keitel soon realized Hitler's motives. There were 750,000 Jews still in Hungary and that country's leader refused to hand them over to Eichmann. Hitler brought the divisions into Hungary, put the leader under arrest, and placed a new government in power, which submitted to his demands. Within four months, most of the Hungarian Jews were rounded up, resulting in the deaths of more than 400,000 men, women, and children. In the meantime, the Russian troops went on to occupy large parts of Prussia. Within one year they took Berlin. It was during this campaign that many German women were raped by Russian soldiers.

"So Adolf Hitler, who spoke so movingly about the sanctity of German womanhood, sacrificed them because of his compulsion to kill Jews."

In the wake of the Holocaust, there is something else that has saddened the rabbi: many Jews, especially survivors, walked away from their religion after the war. With everything they went through, the suffering and anguish, after losing so many family members, many of these survivors had a hard time practicing their faith.

"I would never condemn anyone who suffered and lost faith. I feel sorry for them because religion can make life much more comfortable. Not being religious offers a life that can be filled with doubts, worry, and pessimism about the future. I never doubted G-d's devotion to the Jewish people, but that doesn't mean I understand everything."

The end of the war and its aftermath also created a division among generations.

"For younger people, there was jubilation," recalls the rabbi. "Hitler had been defeated. The evil was destroyed. There would be a new and better world now. But for the older generation, there was a different feeling. Throughout the war, they had hopes that maybe some of their family and friends had escaped. But by 1946, they saw the naked truth. There were so, so many people who hadn't survived."

Rabbi Besser fell in between these two groups. He was both elated *and* haunted. "For two years, I had the same dream almost every night: that I was going to Poland to see our rebbe, but I couldn't find him. So much hope was gone. You suddenly had to erase so many faces from your life."

THE TRIP BACK

Rabbi Besser would go back to Western Europe almost immediately after the war ended, but it wasn't until 1952 that he returned to Germany. It was his first time back since 1933. His family still owned real estate—six buildings in Berlin—and he went there to meet with the woman who managed them, both before the war and after, to assess their condition. It was not an easy trip to make.

"I was very tense, very nervous going back. I was also curious. On the one hand, I didn't expect the proud German people to suddenly look like *sinners going to Canossa* . . . looking for forgiveness. But I wasn't sure how they would react when they saw me."

He flew from Israel to Munich and from there he connected to a flight to Berlin. On the second flight, there were no assigned seats and Rabbi Besser was among the first to board. He sat down in one of the front rows. He remembered having an odd feeling. People came on board, looked at him, were a bit startled, and then quickly moved on. Everyone who followed him tried to sit as far away as possible.

In Rabbi Besser's mind, the reason was simple. "They were not comfortable, I think, with what they had done or what they thought we thought of them because of it."

Finally, the plane was filled and the last person to board *had* to take the seat next to him. After a long wait, the plane finally started up its propellers and departed. As is often the case, neither man said anything to the other. Rabbi Besser had been reading a copy of the *Palestine Post* (the English-language daily that would eventually become the *Jerusalem Post*) since he had just come from Israel. When he finished it and put it down, the man asked: "May I borrow the paper from you?"

"By all means," the rabbi said, happy to hear an American accent.

After a few minutes, the man started up a conversation.

"I see you are from Palestine . . . from Israel," he corrected himself.

And when the rabbi explained that he was indeed traveling from there, the two men began to discuss the military situation. The man spoke admiringly of the Israeli Army and how it had defended itself from so many Arab countries during the recent War of Independence. The man said it was amazing, especially considering the imbalance in numbers. The rabbi, knowing a bit about military campaigns, pointed out that superior numbers don't always determine which side will win. As a case in point, he said, had the Germans held the Allies in Normandy and turned the tide on the Russian front, the smaller German Army might have prevailed.

"So you see," the rabbi told him, "the numbers game is not always relevant."

On military matters, Rabbi Besser was very comfortable and the conversation quickly turned to the strategy of World War II. After they talked for a while, the man asked Rabbi Besser a question.

"If you could name one person responsible for the Allied victory, who would you name?" the man asked.

The rabbi pondered the question for a moment and then answered, "King Peter II of Yugoslavia."

"Please." The man looked at him and replied, "It was a serious question."

"And that was a serious answer," Rabbi Besser responded. He went on to explain.

Hitler's seminal attack on the Soviet Union, code named Barbarossa, was slated to begin in April 1941. But in order to get there, the Germans had to pass through four countries: Hungary, Romania, Yugoslavia, and Bulgaria.

Bulgaria wasn't really necessary to pass through and Hungary and Romania were allies. That left Yugoslavia, which was neutral. Hitler summoned its foreign minister in February, and Germany and Yugoslavia signed a nonaggression pact. Now the road to Moscow was open to the powerful German Army.

In 1936, King Alexander of Yugoslavia had been assassinated in Marseilles. His son, Peter, should have ascended to the throne, but he was underage. So the late king's brother, Pavel, was named regent until the boy was old enough to take the throne. Pavel was much weaker than his brother. The English secret service had a strong presence in Yugoslavia and they were aware of the situation. So they helped orchestrate a coup d'état in Yugoslavia in order to install a government less favorable to Germany.

By this time, Peter was old enough to rule. The uncle was removed. Peter became king and fired the prime minister who had signed the pact with Hitler, invalidating the whole thing. Hitler was so furious, he called in his two commanders in chief, Keitel and Brauchitsch, and told them that Barbarossa would be postponed and they would first attack Yugoslavia. Just out of revenge, Hitler bombed Belgrade, which was not a military target.

So instead of attacking the Soviet Union in April 1941, the Germans attacked Yugoslavia. It took about three weeks to conquer the country and they came to the border of Greece. But the British Army was in Greece. So now Hitler had to attack Greece. And that took another three weeks.

It was now the end of May. The army had to regroup and by the time the Germans could begin the attack on Russia, it was June 22. The original plan called for the capture of Moscow before the winter. The Germans came close—within forty-five miles of Moscow—but because of the delay, they arrived in November, and one of the harshest winters in history stopped them dead in their tracks.

"Had the attack begun in April, as it was originally scheduled," the rabbi explained to the passenger next to him, "they probably would have conquered it before the winter. But because of the three-month delay, Moscow and Leningrad were not captured.

"Because the German Army did not capture Moscow and Leningrad before winter, the entire war began to turn. So if I gave credit to one man, I would give it to King Peter II of Yugoslavia, for changing the outcome of the war by delaying Hitler for a crucial three-month period."

The man in the next seat who had been listening intently to the explanation turned to Rabbi Besser and said, "You know, I never thought of it that way, and I know what you are talking about because I participated."

"What do you mean you participated?" Rabbi Besser was perplexed. "There were no American soldiers there."

"Well," the man smiled, "I'm not an American, I'm German."

"You're German?" the rabbi asked incredulously. "But you speak like an American."

"I studied at Yale," he told the rabbi.

"Before the war?"

"No, after."

Horst Kruger was now a general in the NATO Air Force and would later serve as the German military attaché in Washington. By then, the lights had come on and the plane was landing in Berlin. The conversation came to a natural end, although Rabbi Besser felt uncomfortable with this new information.

As they were gathering their things and leaving the plane, General Kruger looked at Rabbi Besser and said, "I'm German and you are landing in our capital. I feel an obligation as host. Is there anything I could do for you in Berlin while you are here?"

The rabbi thought about it for a moment. Although he was not at peace with what he had learned, he asked for any pictures or films made by the Germans of their war against the Jews. The man clicked his heels and said he would try, and they exchanged cards.

After three or four weeks, a letter arrived from General Kruger. Inside was the name of an archive where he thought the rabbi could find the films he was looking for. There was also something else—a clipping from a German paper about a convention of German officers in which Kruger offered Rabbi Besser's conclusion on the war. When the general told his comrades that he had heard the theory not from a military man but a Jewish rabbi, he said they were shocked.

There is another part to this story that probably says a great deal about both men. In spite of the startling difference in their backgrounds, the general and the rabbi became friends for the next twenty-five years. They visited each other—Rabbi Besser would see him in Washington and Horst Kruger even invited the rabbi to his home near the Swiss border.

The rest of the rabbi's visit proved to be equally interesting and difficult. The last time Rabbi Besser had been in Berlin was six years before the war began. The difference shocked him. Although the rubble had been cleared away by 1952, there were many empty lots where there were once homes and buildings. One of his father's buildings was nothing but a mountain of rubble. The atmosphere was gloomy.

"I stayed in a hotel on the western side. The elevator was broken. In fact, everything seemed to be half-broken."

But there was something about the people that caught his attention.

"Everybody worked," he remembers. "Nobody was sitting in cafés smoking cigarettes, which I saw in Paris. In Germany, I didn't see anyone doing nothing. Even a boy of eight of nine years old was delivering bread—he was doing something to earn some money for his family."

When he came home and was asked his impressions, he told people he would bet on Germany becoming a powerful nation again. It didn't matter how it looked at the time. The fact that this industrious people continued to work so hard in spite of defeat told him that the country would come back again.

When the rabbi met with the woman who had taken care of the family holdings before, during, and after the war, the visit became more emotional. She picked him up at the airport and her first words came out with tears in her eyes.

"I am so ashamed and so sorry," she said with a bowed head.

"She had nothing to be embarrassed about," the rabbi recounts. "She had been a loyal friend and had helped my family. She even risked her life to get money to the Radomsker Rebbe."

But she seemed almost inconsolable. Mrs. D., as they called her, had worked for the Bessers for years. Her real name was Katie Drews. She was meticulous, honest, and loyal. All of the ledgers were presented to the rabbi in intricate detail. Nothing was out of place. Mrs. Drews had a daughter who was a teacher, and the rabbi was interested to find out what German children were learning about the war.

"Nothing," she said. "Nothing."

"We don't talk about it," her daughter explained. "Yes, we know we did something very bad, but nobody wants to discuss it."

"That was more or less the attitude then," remembers the rabbi. "They were not proud and they were not trying to explain. She was not looking forward to talking to me. They were all embarrassed."

There was almost nothing left of the old Jewish community. The German Jews who had not been killed had left, either for America or Israel. There was a very small Jewish presence, but most of these people had come from Eastern Europe, people who had survived the war and decided for one reason or another to stay.

"Many of them became rich and it's nothing to be
proud of," the rabbi says.

Perhaps because of the Germans' guilt, there was now
an overreaction in the other direction toward the few Jews
who remained. Jews received preferential rights and ameni-
ties not available to the rest of the population. Valuable licenses were needed to operate bars and nightclubs and
many of these licenses went to Jews. Since the main source
of barter was cigarettes and most cigarettes were traded in
bars, those who owned bars parlayed this into great, but less
than moral, wealth.

Rabbi Besser himself was offered several impressive,
and legitimate, investment opportunities. Naftali owned six
buildings before the war, three of which were in East Berlin
and considered lost, and three that were in the western sector. One of the buildings, on Bochum Strasse in the American sector, was completely destroyed by bombs. But the lot
was still quite valuable. A builder wanted to put up a large
commercial structure on the block and the family's lot was
right in the middle.

The city of Berlin, wanting to rebuild the city as quickly
as possible in order to further solidify its position against the
Soviets, offered great inducements for anyone who would
build.

"They gave very large mortgages at very low rates. In
this case, all I had was an empty lot. They wanted me to in-
vest 200,000 deutsche marks in the new building and they
offered to add a one-million-mark mortgage at one percent
for forty years."

The proposal became even more valuable when the
builder, eager to make the deal, offered a considerable
amount of money as well. Rabbi Besser quickly calculated

that the building could be constructed without any real investment on his side.

"I soon realized that I could easily purchase other lots for as little as five thousand marks and have buildings constructed with no risk or investment. I could have become a multi-multi-millionaire, without investing anything."

In addition to the real estate, he was also offered the Mercedes-Benz dealership in three states back in America for absolutely nothing—just because he knew someone.

"When I returned home, I told my mother all about it. I felt very satisfied with myself. But someone came to visit—a man I knew very well before the war. His name was Shlomo Leib Bronner and he was a clever man." When the rabbi told him about his business prospects, Bronner, whom Rabbi Besser respected, asked him if he was going to do it.

"Why not?"

Bronner looked at him and then asked, "Do you think G-d let you live—picked you from all of your friends and relatives—to survive the war just so you could get rich and help rebuild Germany? Is that your gratitude?"

"It was like a cold shower," recalls the rabbi.

Rabbi Besser turned down the Mercedes offer immediately. He didn't know the automobile business and probably would have sold the rights anyway. But real estate was something he understood. No matter, he turned down the offer and sold the lot for a relatively cheap price. Within five years, the buildings were worth millions of dollars.

"I don't regret it," the rabbi recalls, almost fifty years later. "I know all the arguments, how you can do good things with a lot of money, but I have no regrets whatsoever."

But the trip left a visible impression on him.

"People saw I was a Jew because of my beard and the way I dressed. They avoided any kind of contact," he remembers. "But I did not feel animosity. I did not feel hatred. I felt embarrassment for them.

"Frankly, I did not encounter the outright anti-Semitism that I experienced many years later in Poland. So it's strange. Here was the country that perpetrated the crime. Poland didn't. Russia didn't. And as soon as the war ended and the evil regime was destroyed, the Germans seemed to go back to their pre-Hitler attitudes toward Jews.

"Almost every Jew who visited Germany after the war—and even today, many decades after the war, always seems to ponder a particular question. Whenever they see someone who would have been of military age at that time, they wonder, What was his role in the war?

"That question is unavoidable. There were so many SS. I would ask myself: Why am I such a polite person to this stranger? This man could have killed my grandfather."

The fact is that the rabbi can't avoid these feelings even today. But he also can't help being a gentleman.

"I have German friends whom I see and feel very good about. They don't have to be embarrassed any more. Still, I think, who knows what someone did back then?"

So the rabbi continues this internal dialogue. He reads everything written on the topic. He talks with people on both sides. And he struggles with it. Sixty years or even one thousand years may not be enough time to understand.

"Perhaps we're still just too close to it all."

SEVEN

THE NEW WORLD

Following a cataclysmic conflict like World War II, everyone might have stopped, caught their collective breath, and reflected on the enormity of what had just transpired. But most people did not. No one had time for the luxury of analysis. Soldiers came home and just wanted to get on with their interrupted lives. The broken countries began to rebuild and the victorious nations jockeyed for greater power in the postwar world. Analysis, it seemed, would be left to historians.

For Jews who suffered such catastrophic losses, the immediate past was also set aside. The focus was on the future, and that future meant building a nation of their own. A dreadfully expensive lesson had been learned and it was not lost on the Zionists. These tough, single-minded political realists were—once and for all—going to create a nation where Jews would never again be dependent on the whims and prejudices of various governments. It would be a place where Jews could come from anywhere, where they would feel at home, and, most of all, where they could defend themselves. And it would be located on the same ground from which they had been uprooted and expelled by the Romans two thousand years before.

The modern political movement that had begun fifty years before the war in Europe by Theodor Herzl started to accelerate.

Many of the wartime alliances quickly fell apart. In Palestine, the British, a staunch ally against Nazi Germany, now stood in the way of a Jewish state. The Arabs, many of whom sided with the Germans but also controlled the oil that the West depended on for its postwar expansion, put pressure on the British to scuttle any Jewish efforts to establish Israel as its once and future homeland. The entire problem would eventually wind up in the United Nations, which was itself in its infancy.

The Jews themselves were divided into three camps. The majority supported the Haganah, the fighting force established by mainstream Zionists. Many in this group were staunch socialists who hoped the Arab world would eventually be swayed toward their political beliefs, creating a socialist utopia in the Middle East. There was the Irgun—the underground group—that used much more radical methods to push out the British and win statehood. Even farther on the fringe was the Stern Gang, which viewed the British as a greater threat than the Arabs. The Stern Gang used any means necessary to oust the British and achieve independent statehood. That often meant violent retaliation for attacks on Jews.

Haskel Besser fell squarely into the more moderate camp—the Haganah. By 1945, he was a young father with obligations to his new family and to his parents and his community. His first child, a son, was born in Tel Aviv on

March 2, 1944. To add to this delight, Shlomo (named after the Radomsker Rebbe) was born on the seventh day of Adar, the birthday of Moses. Haskel and Liba moved into their own home on Hagilboa Street. It was a beautiful apartment with two bedrooms, a dining room, a huge living room, and terraces.

They were only a few blocks from his parents, so they still saw one another several times a day. Naftali did the food shopping for both families. Friday nights and all holidays were celebrated together and the family remained close.

Haskel Besser became Rabbi Besser in 1943. He had begun his rabbinic studies in Europe in 1938 under Rabbi Weiss, the brother-in-law of the Radomsker Rebbe, and continued his studies after his arrival in Palestine with one of the most learned scholars in the Middle East, Rabbi Menachem Zvi Eisenstat. The smicha, or ordination, simply offered a further opportunity to study the Talmud and Torah. Even though he never planned to be a rabbi with a pulpit, he soon became a regular and highly regarded lecturer on Talmud throughout Tel Aviv.

But the Besser family tradition was business, and that is what he gravitated toward. Naftali had always understood that his son grasped things quickly—that's why he could leave him in Poland to tie up his business affairs in 1939 at the age of sixteen. So when Naftali invested in a diamond factory in Tel Aviv after the war, Haskel was trained to run the plant. The factory cut and polished diamonds from South Africa before they were exported to exchanges in Belgium and the United States. He had great success running the business, but he was really more interested in the political events unfolding all around him.

"I think fifty percent of the people who worked in the factory were members of the underground. Some of them later became high officials in the government. By nature, I am a pacifist. Also, I never considered the British to be our enemy. Throughout that period I never felt any fear when I saw British soldiers—except for one night."

That night, the Bessers were at a classical music concert in Ramat Gan, a suburb of Tel Aviv. Before the program had finished, the conductor came on the stage and advised everyone in the audience to go directly home. When the rabbi and his wife arrived back in Tel Aviv, they saw British tanks and military vehicles in the streets. They watched as the British suddenly opened fire, shooting people who were standing nearby.

The Bessers took cover and eventually made it safely to their home. The next day, they learned that the shootings, which killed a number of people, were in reprisal for the killing of British soldiers by the Stern Gang. Strangely, in the middle of all this tumult, it was still possible to have what was in many ways a normal life. Palestine after the war was still a small, very informal country. Everyone seemed to know one another. Rabbi Besser used to see David Ben-Gurion on the street almost every day. The Bessers lived two blocks from Allenby Street, where Ben-Gurion's headquarters were located.

"He stared at me every time he saw me. It was a strange look." The rabbi thinks that was because there were very few Orthodox Jews in Tel Aviv—most were in Jerusalem.

More than ever, postwar Palestine was a mixture of Europe and the Middle East. The climate accommodated an open-air style, which had an impact on Jews from very disparate cultures. The Europeans continued to gather on hotel terraces every afternoon for tea and cakes. Nearby, the loud open markets were much more Oriental. It was all one country and at the same time it was many different countries, with different languages. Everyone seemed to speak Yiddish and German, but you could also hear Russian, Polish, French, Spanish, and Arabic. With the exception of the sabras, everyone struggled with Hebrew.

At the same time, there were millions of people waiting to emigrate. It is now forgotten that within the first few years of the establishment of the state of Israel, a population of 700,000 Jews managed to accommodate an influx of over 2 million more people, many of whom had been expelled from the surrounding Arab lands. Now the population of this fledgling country consisted of Jews from places as diverse as Berlin and Yemen. Israel doubled in size overnight, even while it defended itself from the vastly larger and determined enemy that surrounded it.

THE FIRST JOURNEY WEST

Although the rabbi's health improved after the serious illnesses around his wedding, he still suffered from wrenching headaches. After numerous visits to doctors, the consensus of medical opinion was that it might be the extreme heat that was causing the problem, a cooler climate might improve the situation. The rabbi's sister, Rosa, was now living in New York. She wrote about an outstanding doctor she knew who might be able to help. Suddenly the United States became a viable option. In 1946, Haskel Besser went on a long journey with two goals in mind: he would visit Europe again to see family members who survived the war, and he would make his first trip to America to see the doctor in New York.

"I was very anxious to see our relatives in England, Belgium, Switzerland, and Holland. I wanted to learn more

about what happened to them. And of course, I wanted to
see New York—having seen pictures of it all my life."

Traveling in 1946, within a year of the war, was still difficult. The U.S. Army had not even finished returning all of
its soldiers back to the States, and there were very few flights
that crossed the Atlantic. Ships were still the most common
way to reach America.

The rabbi began his journey with a flight from Tel Aviv
to Cairo. A seat on the TWA flight from Cairo to New York
required not so much a ticket but a bribe to the right person—that's how the travel business worked in Egypt in those
days. The flight, which departed on a Wednesday, should
have taken about twenty hours. But the plane was grounded
in Shannon, Ireland, because of bad weather. This was not
unusual because those early prop planes, with only manual
gears, were more affected by storms and fog.

The passengers were taken to a hotel, but Rabbi Besser
decided to stay in the airport. He didn't want to take any
chance of missing the flight. There was a good reason to be
nervous. With each passing hour, the flight would bring him
closer to Shabbos, and observant Jews never travel between
sundown Friday and sundown Saturday. By Friday morning,
the weather finally improved, and the twenty-five planes that
were held up began flying out one after another. When he
asked what time the plane was due to arrive in New York,
the answer was 11 o'clock at night, well after the start of
Shabbos.

He told the airline ticket officer that he could not
leave.

The officials were astounded.

"Why not?" they asked.

He explained the religious reasons, which didn't seem
to matter to the airline personnel.

"I don't care if you are a saint," he was told, "if you don't leave now, you'll lose your ticket and we won't have space for another six months . . . maybe even eight months."

"I'll take that chance," the rabbi told the officer, making it clear that flying on that plane was simply not an option. There was another religious man traveling with the rabbi, and they asked for the name of a hotel. The officer told him where the people on the flight had stayed the night before and reminded the rabbi that the airline would not pay for it. The rabbi said that he would pay for it and thanked him.

There was a great discussion among the passengers, who had all become acquainted during the long delay. One Jewish man tried to talk the rabbi into leaving with the group—using the logic that since he was just sitting and not *really* working, he wouldn't really be breaking the Sabbath rules. Rabbi Besser explained that if the man wanted to fly, that was his business. But he was not getting on the airplane. Faced with the possibility of a lengthy stay in Ireland, the other passengers expressed their admiration for his convictions. They wished him well and boarded the plane.

On the way to the hotel, the rabbi and his traveling companion stopped to look for any kind of food they could eat over the next day. Kosher food in Ireland in 1946 was not exactly prevalent. All they could find were two items: a can of fruit and a can of condensed milk, both made in Palestine. It was already getting late when they arrived at the hotel and encountered another surprise.

"What are you doing here?" the startled clerk asked. "The hotel is closed for the season."

They had only kept it open for all the passengers who had been grounded, but now that they were gone, the hotel was closed.

The rabbi asked if there were any rooms open at all. "Just for the staff," he was told.

"Let me stay with your staff. I won't ask for anything and after the Sabbath I will leave."

"All right," he was told, "but don't expect anything from us."

But the hotel insisted on at least cleaning his room. Since it was getting late, the rabbi asked if he could go to the room while it was being cleaned in order to prepare for Shabbos. So, facing perhaps months in Ireland and having very little food to see him through the next twenty-four hours, the rabbi headed for his room. When he got there, he noticed two packages that had been left by the man who had stayed there the night before.

"Normally, I would never look inside, but given the circumstances, I decided to take a look."

What he found might be called a miracle of Shabbos. Inside was a large kosher sausage from Tel Aviv along with a bottle of wine. He went down and asked who had occupied the room before him. The clerk looked at the roster. It turned out to be the Jewish man on the plane who tried to talk him into leaving.

"See?" Rabbi Besser says in recounting the story today. "You should always have confidence in the Almighty. It was very good to eat the sausage and have the wine, after eating very little for two days. It probably wasn't the healthiest thing, but never mind."

After the Sabbath ended, there was another surprise. The phone rang at 11 o'clock on Saturday night.

"Mr. Besser?" the caller asked. "We're sending a car to pick you up and you'll be on a flight in two and a half hours."

When the rabbi arrived at the airport, he was told that they had found two available seats on the flight to New York *and* that the car and even the airplane ticket would be picked up by the airline.

"Why?" he asked.

The rabbi remembers their exact words more than half a century later: "Your determination for your religion so impressed us that we wanted to do something."

The rabbi was finally off to New York.

Rabbi Besser loved the Europe of his childhood. He found Palestine close to heaven. But when he came to New York, it was a thrill he had never experienced.

"Such a place! I had never seen anything like this before in my life."

One of the first things that struck this new visitor was the sight of dozens of traffic lights on one of the long avenues in Brooklyn. There were perhaps twenty-five cross streets that the rabbi could see, each with a traffic light alternating between green and red. This is a common sight for anyone who has grown up in an American city, but for the uninitiated, this mundane experience is nothing short of miraculous. He had seen pictures of New York since his childhood, but he wasn't prepared for the grittiness, the dirt, and the ramshackle nature of some of the buildings.

"But I always look at the bright side of things. I liked New York. I liked the people. I liked the way of life very much." And there was one more thing that Rabbi Besser thought separated New York from both Europe and Palestine. "It was the sense of freedom that I especially liked."

The rabbi was now thousands of miles from the devastation of Europe, in a country where, although there were psychic wounds due to the loss of so many soldiers, there was no physical damage from the war. But even in this land of safety and abundance, the pain of the Holocaust wasn't very far from the surface.

On his second Shabbos in America, he went to the Brooklyn home of the Modzicer Rebbe, one of the few Hasidic leaders who survived the war. The last time he had seen this internationally known Hasidic scholar was in the spa town of Marienbad in 1936. This rebbe was famous for his musical compositions and at that last meeting ten years earlier, Rabbi Besser remembered watching as more then ten thousand followers packed in to hear his new melodies written for the high holidays. Ten years later and in the dead of winter, with the lights of both the Shabbos candles and the Chanukah menorah dancing on the walls in the rebbe's home, even the warm glow could not fill the horrible vacuum.

"I looked at the rebbe and thought, just ten years ago, thousands of people strained to see him. And here he was surrounded by maybe fifty people. It was just another reminder of what happened."

He also remembered the rebbe as a powerful figure with a strong, booming voice. Now he looked like a broken man.

"He seemed much, much older," Rabbi Besser remembers. "All he could talk about was what happened, in a soft voice."

Rabbi Besser was able to take some solace in the fact that the rebbe survived. And he saw some other faces that he remembered from the spa visit as well—a visit that now seemed like a century ago.

In his visits and in his general dealings with people throughout his long journey, there always seemed to be a sense of mourning. One could hear it in discussions and see it on the faces of those who survived. Yes, people pushed themselves ahead, but at the same time, they seemed stuck in a dark void. Rabbi Besser visited the doctor his sister recommended and he did manage to cure the headaches. He rented an apartment and even began to look into business opportunities. And he began to struggle with the huge decision of where to live. He loved Israel, but he was fascinated with New York and the possibilities of Jewish life in the United States.

The difficulty in this decision was compounded by the fact that as much as Rabbi Besser loved New York, that's how much Mrs. Besser wanted to stay in Tel Aviv.

On his return trip (by ship this time), although the rabbi didn't realize it at first, he began a project that would continue to this day. He began to collect stories when he stopped in Europe to see what was left and visit those who had survived.

His first stop perplexed him. For the rabbi, the British had been among the greatest heroes of the war, standing up to Hitler at first alone, the only country that seemed to understand the evil threat that the world faced.

"I somehow expected the British to be ten feet tall," he now recalls. "But, of course, they were just normal size. In some cases unimpressive."

He went from England to Belgium and France, all the while collecting stories. People somehow understood that he would listen to them without judgment, and they opened up about such pain that it was hard to imagine how they could live with what they had seen. One man in Belgium told him about Theresienstadt. A woman who had survived Auschwitz was haunted by the faces of the children. Everyone lost family members. Sometimes, the people he spoke to were all that remained of extended families of twenty or thirty human beings.

Rabbi Besser realized that he was, in a sense, a witness. These were stories that should be heard and remembered. He also understood that soon enough, people would forget and, worse, even doubt that such things ever happened. Fifty years before the concept of Holocaust denial even had a name, Rabbi Besser understood that it was one more piece of this immense and tragic puzzle.

Upon his return, he thought he had come up with a solution to his dilemma. The rabbi began commuting between New York and Tel Aviv—staying six months in each city. He established several businesses in the States while he continued his other work in Israel. Liba and the children (a daughter, Aliza, was born in 1948) remained in the apartment on Hagilboa Street. The long separations were difficult and he had a hard time making up his mind where he should settle. His heart was in Israel, but there was also a lack of personal space there that did not fit his personality. In New York, once again, he found the best of both worlds. He could be as Jewish as he wished, and he could also embrace the freedom of America along with the culture of this great metropolis.

Mrs. Besser was adamant in her desire to remain in Israel. In fact, she didn't come to the United States until she was forced to. In 1948, Rabbi Besser had an emergency appendectomy in New York. He asked her to come and she arrived immediately, leaving the children behind to be cared for by relatives. The rabbi concedes that he inadvertently made a huge mistake at the time of his wife's first visit, which didn't help his case. He was subletting an apartment on South Third Street in the Williamsburg section of Brooklyn from a couple that had gone to Florida.

"I was being thrifty and the apartment only cost twenty-three dollars and twenty-five cents a month. But it was terrible, and for a very long time, my wife associated New York with this apartment."

A year before, he had stayed in the lovely apartment of a friend on the West Side of Manhattan, which might have left a very different impression on Mrs. Besser.

He became more involved in the Jewish community of New York, which was now becoming—along with Israel—an epicenter of the Jewish world. He was beginning to take over Naftali's position as head of the family. And like every other Jewish person in the world, he was living in the middle of one of the most important events in the history of his people. He couldn't help getting involved. His arrival in New York coincided with the establishment of the United Nations. One of the first items on its postwar agenda was the debate over the creation of the state of Israel. Rabbi Besser wanted to watch the proceedings and help in any way he could. He managed to attain a press card, but there were certain meetings that were closed to the press.

"It was historic and I wanted to be part of it. I wanted to help, I wanted to be involved." He wanted to be a witness.

The rabbi befriended many of the diplomats in his cordial and knowledgeable manner. He tried to explain that the cause of the Jewish people was just and fair. He also managed to meet some of the leading figures of the early United Nations—Trygve Lie and Andrey Gromyko and two of Stalin's top henchmen, Molotov and Vishynski.

"These were cold Russian bullies, very cold. But Gromyko seemed more approachable. However, one day when I walked up to him, his bodyguards came over quickly and made it very clear that I couldn't talk with him."

The rabbi was actually in Israel when the UN vote on the creation of Israel took place. It happened to fall on a Friday night that was also the birthday of the Husiatiner

Rebbe. Rabbi Besser was going to the Husiatiner Synagogue on that Sabbath. On his way, he passed Mogen David Square in Tel Aviv where tens of thousands of people were gathered to listen to the vote over loudspeakers. After the Friday evening service, the rabbi asked the rebbe if he should go back out to the square to find out the news. It was a serious question because the results were being piped in over the radio and there are very strict rules about not listening to a radio or watching television during Shabbos.

The rebbe looked at him and said, "By all means." So Rabbi Besser went back out to the square, only to find out that the vote had been postponed for another twenty-four hours. Now he would be able to hear the entire event over the radio because it would occur after the Sabbath.

Haskel Besser's own thoughts, dilemmas, and decisions, as well as those of most Jews throughout the world, were suddenly dwarfed by this singular event. After two thousand years of wandering and just three years after the end of World War II, the Jewish people could finally return to their homeland. When Israel became an independent state, he thought that was the end of his personal debate. And yet his time in the United States whetted an appetite for freedom that he had never experienced before.

One of the features of America that impressed Rabbi Besser immediately, and one that most immigrants notice, is the helpfulness of government officials. Often for the first time, they come in contact with bureaucrats who are simply doing their job and don't use their office for bribes or as a demonstration of power. Seeing this for the first time was unlike any experience Rabbi Besser had encountered in his life—from Poland to Germany to Israel—and it enhanced that feeling of freedom he loved in the United States.

"It was a complete freedom that I did not experience in Israel, where you lived under constant supervision of your neighbor. In New York, you could live the way you wished and no one seemed to notice or even care. Not even the people who lived next door, whom you could go for years without even meeting."

He loved the separation of church and state, and how Americans seemed so willing to agree with this, especially after his earlier experiences in Poland where the Catholic Church played such an influential role in political affairs. It was in America that he realized he would be able to live the life he wanted to live. He could live his life as a Hasidic Jew and still be part of a larger, richer, and more complex world. And the more he saw, the more determined he was to become an American, to start a new chapter of his life and leave his old world behind him.

He established a diamond business with a partner—the son of Naftali's partner in Israel. He also started a scrip business, which was an odd outgrowth of the creation of the new Jewish state. Israel, which had ironically been agriculturally bountiful during the war, faced dangerous food shortages partially due to the military conflict with the Arabs. The fledgling Israeli government came up with various remedies. There were many Jewish Americans who wanted to send help, but the Israelis knew that a huge influx of American dollars or British pounds would subvert the effort to establish an independent national economy.

So they set up scrip stores in the United States where people could buy vouchers and send them to relatives in Israel. There, the relatives could exchange them for food in designated stores. Rabbi Besser then took the dollars and bought food from all over the world—meat from South America, sardines from Portugal—to be sent to Israel. Five companies were licensed to sell these scrips. The business flourished for about seven years, until Israel's agriculture and economy began to improve. At that point, the rabbi looked for another business. He always had a good eye for real estate and it was clear to him that compared to the other great cities of the world, prices in New York were low. Almost immediately, he and two partners bought a commercial building in Manhattan.

In 1949, Naftali, who had really not been the same person since he learned about the death of the Radomsk Rebbe, became sick. He went into a hospital in Tel Aviv, and, within a week, he died.

The family was devastated. After the funeral, the rabbi's mother captured the sadness of the day when she said to no one in particular, "Now there is no more Naftali Besser in the world."

"He was more than a man," the rabbi now recalls. "He was a concept. He was so important and did so much and knew so many people."

Naftali Besser was a popular personality in Europe and was known by thousands of people. He was a paragon of honesty and respectability. In these regards, his son was not unlike him. But Naftali seemed to be permanently damaged by the war. He had escaped but was haunted by everything that had happened. Perhaps because he was younger, perhaps because he was different, Rabbi Besser's reaction was not the same. While he has spent his life trying to understand what happened, he was not debilitated by it. After Naftali's death, Rabbi Besser decided to move the family to the United States. There would always be a strong connection with Israel, but in many ways, he understood that if Judaism were to be rebuilt after its greatest disaster, its rebirth would take place in both Israel *and* America.

Eight

"Go See Besser"

In 1949, Haskel Besser brought his wife and two young children to the United States. His mother would follow soon after, along with his brother, Akiva. His sister, Rosa, was there already.

The Bessers first found an apartment in the Hasidic section of Brooklyn. From the start, they needed more space, and three years later, in 1952, he discovered the apartment on Riverside Drive. He fell in love with it immediately and, without waiting for Liba's approval but knowing her taste, he signed a lease on the spot. It is the home they have lived in ever since.

Manhattan may have seemed an unusual choice since the epicenter of the Hasidic community in New York was Brooklyn. But for Haskel and Liba, who loved the West Side, it made perfect sense. The neighborhood was certainly Jewish in its makeup. There were kosher restaurants and stores within walking distance. There were shuls on practically every other block. They lived directly across the street from a beautiful park where the rabbi liked to stroll. But perhaps what Haskel Besser liked best was the chance to replicate parts of the old world he knew as a boy.

Many of the Jewish immigrants who managed to get out of Europe and settle in Manhattan in the '30s and '40s came from large cities of great culture—Berlin, Vienna, and Budapest. These highly educated people, often from wealthy backgrounds, brought a cosmopolitan lifestyle with them and, like all immigrants before and after, made their own very distinct mark on the elastic fiber of New York. Viennese coffeehouses served this new clientele. There were Hungarian restaurants, European bakeries, and candy stores run by couples with strong accents. The chess club on the West Side was filled with many of these immigrants. The recent arrivals became regulars at the Metropolitan Opera, Carnegie Hall, and the city's museums.

New York was perfect for this revival because it was one of the few cities in America where people still actually walked. On Saturday mornings, families dressed in their best suits strolled to shul. After lunch, they had their shpatsiers—afternoon strolls—just like the walks they took with their parents in Europe before the war.

These people were distinctly different from their American-born neighbors, and it wasn't just their accents that set them apart. Their dress was often more formal. There was a certain tidiness compared to their more casual neighbors. For the Bessers and other Orthodox Jews, there was another advantage to living on Manhattan's West Side. The population of Poland before the war was 10 percent Jewish. Although that number was much lower throughout the United States (less than 2 percent overall), New York City had the highest concentration of Jews in the world at that time (25 percent—2 million out of a total population of

8 million), which made the new immigrants immediately comfortable. There was a Jewish sense that seemed to permeate the entire city.

When Rabbi Besser first went to look at the apartment that would become his home, he took note of the shtibel across the street.

"I always liked convenience, and in Manhattan, everything seemed to be available at any hour of the day or night and it was all within reach."

SETTING UP SHOP

While it's true that Rabbi Besser came from a wealthy family, his was also a family that believed in hard work. He had opened an office on Rivington Street on the Lower East Side in 1946 and moved to midtown in 1950 to a building on Forty-fifth Street, between Fifth and Sixth Avenues—just five subway stops from his home. His business partner, Lew Shulgasser, was a perfect match. Shulgasser was happy to take an active role in running the business, which focused on commercial real estate, while Rabbi Besser offered his capital but spent more and more of his time helping people and lecturing. This soon became his focus. Although Shulgasser was Jewish, he wasn't as religious as the rabbi and he seemed content to help his people by allowing the Rabbi more time to devote to these matters. Both men trusted each other and the business flourished. They eventually were involved in office buildings as far west as Seattle.

"Go see Besser." It was a familiar phrase within New York's Orthodox community beginning in the 1950s. Word had begun to spread that there was a man who would listen to a problem and, more times than not, come up with a solution. People came with a wide variety of questions and problems ranging from historic debates to personal difficulties: A woman on the West Side, heartbroken because she could not conceive a child after ten years of marriage. A man unsure when he should hand out money for charity on Purim because the holiday fell on Shabbos that year. A couple having marital problems. A lady in Cleveland wanting to know if she can move her mother's body, which is buried in Romania, to be next to her father's grave in Israel (the answer is yes—a body can be reburied, but only in Israel).

The rabbi never advertised his services and he never turned anyone away. It often kept him from the things he needed to do, and it also kept him from studying the Torah and Talmud.

"But it was always interesting," he says, putting his usual positive spin on a vocation that he seemed to stumble into. "Of course, there are times I wish the phone would stop ringing," he says. This is surprising, because whenever he answers, at any time of the day or night, his voice is always cheerful, as if he had been just waiting for that call.

"Most people have a weakness," he notes, "and this is mine: I can't say no."

If he is out for a day or two, there can be as many as seventy messages waiting for him in his office—often from people he has never met. Although the questions vary, the rabbi has noticed that the subtext of the problems has shifted with the times.

"Thirty or forty years ago, many people struggled with religious questions and the Shoa [Holocaust]," recalls the rabbi. "If the people were sincere, I tried to explain my views, not to persuade them to think the way I thought but because I saw they were struggling and I thought this might help."

That is the other factor that brings people cascading into his life—the rabbi is a very good listener. He rarely interrupts and has a natural ability to see beyond what the person is asking in order to find the real reason the person is seeking advice. This special quality makes him not unlike a good psychiatrist and has brought some rather unusual stories his way.

THE SOVIET JOURNEY

In the same office building on Forty-fifth Street, there was a travel agency called Cosmos, run by one Gabriel Reiner. One day in 1955, Reiner came into the rabbi's office and asked what seemed to be an unusual question.

"Besser," he called out, "can you help me? I need to know when Shabbos is next month in Helsinki."

He told Reiner he could certainly find out. But Rabbi Besser knows that a question like that can be a lead-in to an even more intriguing story. "Tell me the whole problem," he added.

Reiner explained that a chess tournament between the United States and Russia would take place in Moscow in the summer and he was in charge of making the travel arrangements. The number one player in the United States at the time was Samuel Reshevsky, an Orthodox Jew, who observed the Sabbath. Reiner wanted to know when Reshevsky could and could not travel. This was 1955, and travel visas to the Soviet Union were extremely hard to obtain. Stalin had died just two years before. It was one of the darkest periods of the cold war. The chess foray was one of the first cultural exchanges between the United States and the Soviets.

"This is really interesting," the rabbi told Reiner. "Tell me about it. How many people are going?"

"Sixteen," said Reiner. "Seven players and three reserves in case someone gets sick. That's ten, a referee from our side and the president of the association, that's twelve, plus four assistants, that's sixteen."

"Well, if sixteen can go," said the rabbi, "why not seventeen?"

"Do you want to go?" asked Reiner.

"No, I can't go," the rabbi answered. "I don't look like a chess player at all. But why don't you go? You speak Russian. You are from there. It's impossible to get a visa, and you have one in your hand."

"You know, Besser, I never thought of that. I'll ask my wife."

On the rabbi's suggestion, Reiner was off to the Soviet Union. The rabbi forgot about the incident until, one day about eight weeks later, Reiner came back into his office.

"What was strange was that Reiner was wearing a coat. It was August by then, and I asked him where he was coming from."

"From the airport," explained Reiner.

"From Russia?" asked the rabbi.

"No, from Washington," said Reiner. "I went from Russia to Washington to speak to someone at the State Department and gave them a full report. Now I'm here. You are the first man I am coming to see after the State Department. I want to tell you what happened to me."

Gabriel Reiner explained that after the group's arrival in Russia, his participation quickly seemed to be a big mistake. The trip was a monumental bore. Although he could speak the language, no one was allowed to go anywhere alone—they were all under constant supervision. Reiner wanted to see two things: the Hermitage museum and Suwalki, the small town in Poland where he was born, but he quickly found out both were off limits. Reshevsky won his match, but the Russians won all the rest. Needless to say, the Soviets were quite pleased with the event and it dominated the local press.

On the Fourth of July, the U.S. embassy invited the group of Americans to its Independence Day celebration. But even here, Reiner felt out of place. There was no one to talk to, only the chess group and some diplomats from other embassies. So after a few drinks, he thought: enough celebrating, time to go. Just as he was about to leave, the embassy doorbell rang and in walked the entire Soviet government.

Leading the delegation was Nikita Khrushchev. When the group walked in, they just stared at everyone and everyone stared at them. No one seemed to quite know what to do. The U.S. ambassador was not there (he was in Washington at the time) and the chargé d'affaires was in the other room.

Reiner said that Khrushchev, who was loud and rude at times, said in a husky voice in Russian, "Ah, nobody is here to greet us. Nobody will even say hello. I see."

Reiner looked around. No one said a word. So he took it upon himself to walk over and reply in Russian, "Welcome, welcome, please come in," and offer all of them a drink. Eventually, embassy protocol took over and Reiner once again receded into the background.

But after a short time, Khrushchev came over to him.

"Can you drink?" Khrushchev asked. This was not a question but a challenge.

Reiner told Rabbi Besser that he actually thought he *could* drink, so the two men sat down and the vodka started to pour. Reiner quickly discovered he was completely out of his league. He watched in amazement as Khrushchev downed twenty-seven shots of vodka. Twenty-seven! And he only seemed to be warming up.

"Tell me," Khrushchev said. "What are you doing here? Who are you? You're not Russian. You're an American, but you speak Russian. You must be a spy."

"I'm a travel agent," Reiner replied.

"A travel agent?" he asked. "How did you get to Moscow?"

"I organized the chess tour," he told Khrushchev.

"You're with the chess tournament?" Khrushchev asked with his eyes widening. "Is Reshevsky here?"

"Yes," Reiner told him.

Khrushchev suddenly got excited and asked to meet him. He said he wanted to have his picture taken with him. So Reshevsky was brought over to Khrushchev and photographers began snapping pictures. Reshevsky was a small, quiet man who seemed quite uncomfortable with the entire encounter.

Khrushchev went back over to sit with his new friend, Reiner, and he began asking questions. Was he married? Did he have children? Reiner said yes to both and added that his son was in the army.

"Where is he?" asked Khrushchev.

"Not far from here," said Reiner. "He's in Berlin."

That sent Khrushchev into a tirade on the East-West confrontation. Why was Reiner's son in Berlin? What business did the United States have in Berlin? Reiner thought about this and an idea suddenly came to him. Perhaps it was the vodka that emboldened him to even suggest it but he said he could actually help Khrushchev and the Soviet Union in their struggle to be better understood in the world.

Reiner explained that during his trip, he did not meet one Russian who was not affected by the war in one way or another. Almost everyone had lost a family member or knew someone who had been killed or wounded. Everyone he met spoke about the war with great sadness.

"They are still very upset about it and they certainly don't want another one," said Reiner. "But people in the United States don't know this. You should convince Americans that you don't want a war with us."

"And how can we do that?" asked Khrushchev in a slightly sarcastic tone.

"You should open your gates to American tourists. Right now you allow in maybe one or two tourists a year. But a million tourists would come back with stories of what life is really like. And that could change the world . . . to say nothing of the fact that they would bring millions of American dollars."

"What's your name?" Khrushchev asked.

"Reiner."

"You must be a Jew," remarked Khrushchev as he motioned to a man standing nearby. "This is Anastas Mikoyan, my economic adviser."

And then Khrushchev directed his comments to his advisor.

"Reiner has a proposal to make that I agree to. You meet with him. Make an agreement with him tomorrow. Reiner is in charge. He is the only one who has my permission."

Then Khrushchev turned to Reiner and said in a lower voice, "You Jews think you are the smartest people in the world. Mikoyan is Armenian. When you leave his office, count your fingers. *They* are much smarter than you."

Then the drinks really began to affect Khrushchev. He became friendlier and more open.

"Do you know why I like you?" Khrushchev said to Reiner. "You are a simple man. I bet you never graduated from school, did you?"

"No," replied Reiner.

"Neither did I," said Khrushchev. "You see my colleague over there [motioning to Nikolai Bulganin], he graduated from Frunze Academy [the Soviet West Point]. He wears white gloves and thinks he's superior to everyone else. I bet I have more in my heel than he has in his whole head."

Then with great bravado, Khrushchev asked if there was anything at all Reiner desired to do while he was in Russia. Reiner thought about this for a moment and then said, "I would like to see the Hermitage."

"Who's stopping you?" asked Khrushchev.

"I've been asking all week long, and all week, all I've heard is nyet."

"Tomorrow," Khrushchev said pounding his hand on the table, "you go to the Hermitage. But there must be something else you want, isn't there?"

"Well," said Reiner. "I was born in a town called Suwalki. I was only a child when I left, but I'd like to see it again. I remember it was the nicest city I've ever seen."

"Where is Suwalki?" asked Khrushchev.

"It's in Poland," said Reiner.

"So why can't you go?" asked Khrushchev.

"The Polish consulate won't give me a visa," he replied.

"You go to the consulate tomorrow," said the Soviet leader, "and you tell them Khrushchev sent you and said they should give you a visa."

The next day, Reiner woke up early and couldn't wait until he got to the Polish consulate. When he walked in and asked for a visa, the woman behind the counter asked him where he lived.

The Fourth of July party at the U.S. embassy in Moscow, 1955. The small man in the center is the U.S. chess champion, Sam Reshevski. To the right, Nikita Khrushchev. To the left, Nikolai Bulganin, followed by Lazar Kaganovitsh, Stalin's brother-in-law, with his arm on Gabriel Reiner. *(From* Life *magazine, July 7, 1955. Photo by Leonard McComb/Time Life Pictures/Getty Images. All rights reserved.)*

"New York," Reiner told him.

Almost with disdain, the woman waved him off. "You will have to apply in the United States," he was told.

"Yes," said Reiner. "But the consulate in the States wouldn't give me one and Khrushchev said you should give me a visa."

"Who?" asked the consul. "Khrushchev? We get our orders from Warsaw . . . from the Ministry of Foreign Affairs. They tell us who to give visas to."

And that was that. Reiner went back to the hotel feeling foolish and thought: *Yesterday was a fantasy. We were drunk last night and great friends, but today it doesn't mean a thing.* But shortly after he returned to his room the phone rang.

"Hello?" asked the caller. "Are you the gentleman who came by the Polish consulate?"

"Yes."

"Would it be possible for you to stay at your hotel for another half hour?" the caller asked.

"Yes," said Reiner again. "I have no place else to go."

Within a half hour, two men arrived at his room and began to apologize.

"The person you spoke with didn't understand what exactly it was that you were saying. Where is your passport? We wish to give you the visa, but you must tell us when you are coming because you are the guest of the Polish government. They must know when you are coming."

Later, another man appeared in the hotel with three lawyers to work out a deal giving Reiner sole control in the United States for tourist visas to Russia and he added something else: Reiner would also have control over all parcels sent to Russia from the United States.

The following day, he went to the Hermitage. The day

after that, Reiner boarded a train to Warsaw where he was greeted by an entire delegation.

As he finished his story in the rabbi's office, Reiner wanted to show his appreciation for his good fortune, which seemed to fall into his lap. He wanted to share this business deal with Rabbi Besser since it was the rabbi who encouraged him to go in the first place.

It was a lucrative offer. The rabbi thanked him but did not accept it. Reiner had a monopoly on travel to the Soviet Union for about a year, until other tour operators began to protest the agreement. But he didn't seem to mind. According to Rabbi Besser, he had no problem sharing.

"Besides," the rabbi says, "he had a great story that he told over and over for many years."

Rabbi Besser sees a geopolitical element to this story as well. The rabbi thinks that by opening up its borders and eventually allowing Soviet citizens to see Westerners, ordinary people within the Soviet Union began to see their vastly different standard of living—in spite of what they were told by their state-run media. The exposure to outsiders gave people courage to protest and that led to the refuseniks. The refuseniks led to Gorbachev. And that led to the collapse of the Soviet Union.

"You know," the rabbi muses, "I prayed that Communism would end but not by a military defeat. If it happened that way, people would have blamed the end of Communism on the victors. I always hoped it would collapse on its own and I was very pleased when it did. I like to think that maybe I had a small part in the process."

THE FORGOTTEN MAN

There are very few history books that contain the name Emil Sommerstein. But before the war, he was one of the most famous Jewish lawyers in Poland, known for his willingness to take on any case that would help Jews, Zionism, and the creation of the state of Israel.

Sommerstein spent the war in a Russian prison. Afterward, he was elected to the Polish government for a brief time. In the late 1940s, Sommerstein came to the United States to speak at a large rally for Israel in Madison Square Garden. Hundreds of people stood in line to shake his hand. Shortly after that event, he suffered a stroke and was hospitalized in the United States, alone and forgotten. All of those people who stood in line to shake his hand were oblivious to his plight. He spent his days in his daughter's home about forty miles north of New York City in the Catskill Mountains. He would have died unnoticed, except for a graceful gesture on the part of Rabbi Besser.

"I had never met him," said Rabbi Besser, "but I admired him very much. His speeches were very elegant, his arguments forceful."

Rabbi Besser knew someone else who was concerned about Sommerstein and, since the rabbi had a car, they began to visit him regularly.

"His mind was still perfect, but his body was almost paralyzed. We had very interesting conversations."

One day, Sommerstein's name came up in a conversation with Elie Wiesel who asked if he could come along on one of the visits. After the visit, the rabbi, Wiesel, and a visiting Israeli drove back from the Catskills and talked about the man, what he had done, and how he was now forgotten.

The rabbi observed aloud that Israel wasn't always

proficient at honoring people who had worked so hard on its behalf. "If Sommerstein were a Frenchman or Italian, his chest would have been covered with medals," said the rabbi. And he asked if there wasn't some way to recognize this man who was now more than eighty years old and in poor health. The visiting Israeli agreed and said he would see what he could do.

Six weeks later, the rabbi received a call from the Israeli consul general who informed him that a package had arrived for him from Israel. He asked the consul to open it, and inside was an award for Sommerstein.

"A big megillah [deal] . . . signed by some very important people," the consul told him.

The rabbi was pleased. He explained that the consul should present this award personally to Sommerstein.

"No problem," said the consul. "Where does he live?"

When the rabbi told him it was about forty miles north of New York, the consul demurred.

"Forget it," she said. "Why don't you give it to him yourself?"

"But my giving it is not valid. I'm not an Israeli citizen. You're the Israeli consul," the rabbi replied.

"All the powers vested in me," the consul told the rabbi over the phone, "I now give to you for this instance." The rabbi was now a temporary official of the state of Israel.

The rabbi then called Sommerstein's daughter to tell her the news because he was afraid it would be a shock for him if he just arrived without warning. When the day came, Rabbi Besser drove up and brought along some extra people "to make it more festive." Sommerstein was waiting for him. He was sitting up in bed in new pajamas and a new bathrobe.

"My dear rabbi," Sommerstein told Rabbi Besser as he entered the small room, "I am prepared for my ceremony."

"I played my role very well," Rabbi Besser remembers with great pride. "I said: In the name of the prime minister and the Israeli cabinet—I even added a few lines."

Tears were streaming down Sommerstein's face and he kissed the rabbi on both cheeks.

"Now I can die in peace," Sommerstein said.

"It was so moving," remembers Rabbi Besser more than fifty years later. "It shows what a little bit of kindness can accomplish."

A FULL PARTNER

In 1953, Haskel Besser became a citizen of the United States. Like everything else he does, he took his citizenship test seriously and made sure he was prepared for it. Perhaps the judge who administered the test noted a touch too much confidence in the rabbi, as he asked him who was the first president to be born in the United States. The rabbi looked a little nervous as he searched his memory for the answer.

Upon seeing his concern, the judge leaned over and told him: "It was Martin van Buren. But don't worry, no one else here knows it either."

He has voted in every election since that day, without missing one. He wears an American flag on his lapel. The rabbi has loved his trips across the United States, visiting cities, national parks, and even Disneyland. "I liked it, but my children liked it more."

In 1955, his second daughter, Debbie, was born. And in 1958, his fourth child, Naftali, arrived. The apartment was filled with children and it was Mrs. Besser who had the traditional role of raising them. Rabbi Besser was often traveling,

Crossing the Atlantic in 1953 aboard the *Queen Elizabeth,*
with Liba and their two children at the time, Shlomo and
Eliza. *(Family photograph)*

but still, the children are completely devoted to their father,
who they view with a certain degree of awe, respect, and
great love.

It was Shabbos and holidays when the family came together. The clocks seemed to stop and no matter how busy
things were during the week, each child had time with the
rabbi.

When his eldest son, Shlomo, was fifteen years old, he
was sent to study at a yeshiva in Cleveland, Ohio. This is in
keeping with a Hasidic tradition that comes from the Talmudic edict: Hevei gola limkom Torah, which loosely translated means "If you want to learn, you better leave home."

Rabbi Besser skiing in St. Moritz, January 1960.
(Family photograph)

"A child is used to his mother, his home, and his habits," the rabbi explains. "But we believe that in order to pay more attention to studies, he should get away from such luxuries. It also makes children more mature."

Even though rebellion tore many American families apart in the 1960s, the Besser family experienced none of it. And the Rabbi says that is tied directly to their strong belief system.

"I think there is less rebellion in children in religious homes because we are happy with our past," Rabbi Besser observes. "Most of the world wants reform because they think they are more advanced than those who came before. Religious Jews believe the opposite—that our fathers and their fathers were wiser.

"We believe that the Torah was given to the Jews on Mount Sinai and this was our pinnacle. Every year since then, we have progressively diminished as a people.

"If you believe this, and Hasidim do, then you realize the basis for respect for parents: they came first and therefore they know more and whoever knows more should be respected. This also explains why our rebbes and sages are reluctant to criticize a commentary on Talmud that came three or four hundred years earlier because the first writers are closer to the event."

The rabbi will readily agree that there are exceptions to this rule on both sides. There are nonreligious families where children show great respect for their parents, and there are some religious families with terrible problems. And as for childhood rebellion, the rabbi understands that this can be a natural part of the growth of a personality. He has nothing against it.

"A person should establish his identity, and doing so with force shows character," he admits. "I did so myself."

Since Rabbi Besser always speaks of his parents with such loving respect, one must wonder how this rebellion manifested itself.

"I did things differently," he says. "I sang my songs and recited my prayers differently."

"You don't want too much change," he advises. "Just a little."

THE LIAR

As the world moved farther from the Holocaust, the questions posed to the Rabbi changed as well. In some ways, people were moving on. But the problems associated with the event never ceased.

In the 1960s, a mutual acquaintance sent a couple to talk with Rabbi Besser. The German government wanted to stop paying them reparations and, worse, they wanted six years of back pay because of a fraudulent item that was found on their original application. The rabbi listened to the whole story and came up with a plan. He said he had heard a good word about the new German consul, Dr. von Kotzebue, and although he had never met her, he would see if he could discuss the matter with her.

About a week later, Rabbi Besser was ushered into the consul's office where she greeted him and offered him a cup of coffee. The consul immediately showed a great understanding of Jewish practice by asking her assistant to be sure that the coffee was in a glass (the only way someone who keeps kosher will drink outside his home). The rabbi showed the German consul the papers that the man had submitted and she read them over thoroughly. Afterward, she said it was very clear: "Paragraph seven states that if you give fraudulent testimony, you forfeit your right to any funds. The man gave fraudulent information. That's that."

"May I tell you a story?" the rabbi asked.

"By all means," she replied.

And the rabbi began to tell the man's story, which was, in many ways, the story of thousands of others.

"The man in this document lived in a city called Skarzysko in Poland. One day in 1941, a German police car went through the town with a loudspeaker and commanded that all Jews in the town gather in the main square. If they didn't, they'd be shot.

"So all the town's three thousand Jews gathered in the square at the appropriate time. The soldiers in charge let them stand there for seven to eight hours—first in the hot sun, and then in the cold rain—just to break any resistance in them.

"Then an officer in polished boots and a crisp uniform spoke at the head of the group. He said all children up to fifteen should move to the right. Everyone fifteen to fifty-five should stand in the middle, and everyone older than fifty-five should move to the left.

"The man in question was fourteen years old at the time and should have moved to the right, but his instinct told him to move in with the middle group. At that moment, this man committed his first lie, which also happened to save his life that day.

"On the following day, everyone in the middle group was asked if they had any vocational training. And even though he was just a schoolboy, he followed his instincts and raised his hand again, committing another lie. And again another door to life opened.

"The following day, after standing in a long line, he was asked by a man with a pen and a long list what exactly his vocation was. He said he was a cook, although he didn't know how to boil water. Over the next four years, this boy who should have been in school and playing games was, instead, learning to survive by lying.

"In the most important years of his life when he should have been maturing into manhood, he learned that the only way to stay alive was by lying, and he will never be cured from what was imprinted on him. Whose fault is it that he will lie all his life?"

Pointing his finger at Dr. von Kotzebue, he said: "It's you Germans and you should be liable for this all his life. Is it fair? Do you call this justice?"

The consul looked at the rabbi with an expression that showed him that she understood. She asked him a question in German.

"Rabbi," she asked, "where did you study law?"

"I never studied law," the rabbi told her. "I only studied Talmud."

"I am a professor of law," she replied. "I could immediately certify you as an able jurist."

Although she had no jurisdiction over this matter, she told the rabbi to tell the couple they had nothing to worry about.

"She was a remarkable woman," the rabbi remembers. "We became friends forever. She even came to me for advice."

These two people could have been adversaries. They certainly were at odds when the rabbi walked into the consulate. But Rabbi Besser not only brings opponents around to his point of view, but befriends them as well.

A COMMITMENT

Rabbi Besser is not necessarily a joiner of clubs, but there is one organization that he has been involved with for almost fifty years. It is called Agudah, which comes from the biblical Hebrew meaning "to bind together." The organization was founded in 1912 as an Orthodox response to the growing political power of secular Judaism. The three other Jewish organizations at the time, which were attracting large followings, had little to do with religion. They were the Zionists, who were working for the creation of a Jewish homeland in Palestine, the Bund, made up of Jewish socialists and labor groups, and the Mizrachi, a religious offshoot of the Zionists, but further to the left than Agudah.

Religious Jews organizing themselves into a political unit was an unusual move. It was clearly a reaction to the modern world as religious Jews were reluctant to make changes or reform their practices. A group of about three hundred highly respected religious leaders gathered in Katowice to create Agudah in hopes of giving religious Jews a voice and some influence on world events that impacted the Jewish people. They included the Gerer Rebbe, Rabbi Chaim Soloveichik of Brisk, Rabbi Chaim Ozer Grodzinski of Vilna, Rabbi Jacob Rosenheim of Frankfurt, and Rabbi Israel Freedman of Chortkov.

The first major convention was planned for 1914 in Switzerland but was canceled because of the outbreak of World War I. When he was fourteen years old, during the summer of 1937, Haskel Besser and his family attended an Agudah conference in Marienbad. He was able to hear some of the greatest Talmudic scholars in the world and remembers being fascinated. But world events again overtook the organization, and Rabbi Besser would not become in-volved in Agudah until after he moved to America.

In 1953, on the advice of the organization's president, Rabbi Yitzhak Mayer Lewin, whom Rabbi Besser had known since childhood, Haskel Besser joined Agudah and was elected a vice president at his first conference. He has been a major force in the organization ever since, concentrating his efforts on, among other things, the Talmud. In 1958, an-other rabbi, Mendel Kasher, came to Rabbi Besser and asked that he help organize a daily Talmud class like the ones in Europe before the war. Although there had been two small groups reading the Talmud in Brooklyn, the prac-tice of reading daily had not caught on with American Jews. Rabbi Besser had enjoyed reading the Daf Yomi (a page a day) back in Poland, but the complex and intricate nature of the Talmud makes the daily reading not just an exercise but a commitment.

"I thought it was a good idea," recalls the rabbi, "al-though I had doubts that this kind of study would catch on in the United States."

The rabbi first went to a friend, Rabbi Henry Wolf, who had a nearby congregation on the Upper West Side, and suggested they hold a nightly class, seven days a week. But they had a difficult time finding someone to lead it—it is a huge time commitment to teach Talmud. They resolved to divide up the responsibilities between six different people including Rabbi Besser and Rabbi Wolf. Each man would take one night and a special guest would be brought in on Friday nights. The class caught on by word of mouth and soon there were nine different classes in synagogues on the West Side. The first celebration of the completion of the Tal-mud took place in the mid-sixties and was attended by sev-eral hundred men.

Back then, Rabbi Besser was puzzled by something he observed in America. There were millions of young Jewish men and women who attended some of the finest universities in the country. They studied everything from law and medicine to history, math, and Greek philosophy. But the vast majority didn't touch Torah studies. They were learning about everything except their own heritage.

Rabbi Besser is deeply concerned that many young American Jews move to other faiths and politics not because they disagree with Jewish philosophy, but because they are ignorant of it.

"If you don't like it, it's too bad. But at least you should know what you don't like."

Even though he thought young people could find inspiration in the Talmud, he could not imagine how this could happen, since it is written in Aramaic, a language quite foreign to the vast majority of Jews in the United States.

In the late sixties and early seventies his eldest daughter, Aliza Grund, noticed a change in the Besser home. Throughout her childhood, the Besser table was a gathering place for some of the most learned and respected Jewish intellectuals in the world.

"It was not unusual to come home on Shabbos and find Elie Wiesel or a group of brilliant scholars like Adin Steinsaltz along with famous rabbis and diplomats at the table," she remembers.

But after their children left home and began their own families, Rabbi and Mrs. Besser opened up their home and their Shabbos table to any young person who was interested in learning what Shabbos was all about. Here was one of the most learned Jewish couples in America welcoming even the most rudimentary questions about their religion.

"I was quite surprised to learn that my mother had signed a list at a very popular West Side synagogue offering to host anyone who wanted a place to go on Shabbos," she remembers. "My parents' home became less exclusive as they opened it up, but there was something very nice about that."

By the 1980s, as the baby boomers began to age, many started to realize their ignorance of their own religion. They may have needed more grounding and they also realized that they wanted to pass on some religious training to their children. Manhattan synagogues that were dying in the 1960s and 1970s suddenly witnessed a remarkable turnaround.

This was a generation in which many chose to reject a great deal of what they were given—materialism, social rules, and religion. Whether it was a search for spirituality or focus, or just a way to meet a partner, many young Jews began coming back to the fold. Many came back to Conservative or Reform synagogues. But there were others who became baalei teshuvah (masters of repentance), those who return to the Orthodox fold.

A new generation of Jews began seeking ways to learn about and practice their religion. Many synagogues that could barely make a minyan (ten people) were suddenly filled to overflowing on Friday nights. So it was in this period of return that Talmud study began to grow in popularity.

Rabbi Besser came up with the idea of producing small editions of the Talmud that could be easily carried while commuting. Being realistic, he knew how busy most people's lives are these days. He knew that spending several hours every day studying the Talmud, as was done in Europe, is really not a possibility for most American Jews. So he pushed the idea of reading just one page a day.

Since he believes time is one of our most precious gifts

and must not be wasted, Rabbi Besser has pondered how every moment can be used to its fullest. He once calculated that most people spend a minimum of one hour a day waiting, whether it's in traffic or in a bank line or in a restaurant. That's seven hours a week, fifteen days a year, which comes to over two years of waiting in the course of a normal lifetime. That's where the pocket-sized volume of the Talmud comes in.

"Why not study and learn," asks the rabbi, "rather than just sit on a subway and listen to the sound of the train?"

The rabbi is also realistic in another way. He understands that a person cannot be forced to learn. "That creates a reaction against it. People for the most part don't like to be told what to do, what to learn, or what to think."

So he still had his doubts that this would ever really catch on.

ArtScroll, a Jewish publishing house, did what might seem to be the impossible—they translated the Talmud and made it easier to read. There are also websites with the day's passage along with explanations. Agudah even created a telephone service in which one can hear the latest chapter in English or Yiddish any time, day or night. Suddenly all over Manhattan and across the country, Jews young and old began studying the Talmud.

"Now they are learning not because they have to but because they want to. And this type of learning is much more important than learning by force. It stays with you."

All of this culminated on an early fall night in 1997 in, of all places, Madison Square Garden. The Garden was filled with over twenty thousand men—dressed in dark Hasidic garb and fedoras (another seventy thousand around the world watched the event on closed-circuit television).

They were all there to celebrate the completion of the

Rabbi Besser addressing a full house at Madison Square
Garden in 1997, on the occasion of the completion of
reading the Talmud at one page a day. *(Agudah Israel
Archives)*

reading of the Talmud, which, at the rate of a page a day,
takes seven and a half years. The number of people alone
was astounding, but the fact that this event was held in the
United States offered further proof that the center of the
Jewish world had shifted.

And sitting in the middle of the main table with a group
of distinguished rabbis on the stage was one of the guiding
forces behind this movement—Rabbi Haskel Besser.

Rabbi Besser has a keen awareness of the future of Orthodox Judaism. Since the end of the war, he understood
that the United States offered a unique opportunity in the
long history of the Jewish people.

"In the 1970s I went to the Bobover Rebbe's shul in

Brooklyn and I saw an amazing sight: thousands of people, young people, all dressed as they were in Poland, all living lives as pious Jews. So you *can* bring it back, just not in Europe." He thinks Europe will always have a Jewish presence, but it will never again be what it was before the war.

Rabbi Besser is optimistic about Judaism's future in America. If headlines in Jewish newspapers bemoan the high intermarriage rate and the low birthrate among younger American Jews (both quite true), the rabbi can still look at the glass and see it half full. Yes, it troubles him when he sees people abandoning their faith, but he also has the capacity to be amazed with every baal teshuva he meets.

"In Poland before World War II, the Jews had no alternative. They were not allowed to assimilate into Polish society. Here in the United States, there is freedom no one has ever known. And still these people choose this much more difficult life. This should not be overlooked."

A FRIENDSHIP

It was through Agudah that Rabbi Besser met perhaps his closest friend. Although he first met Moses Sherer years before, when he first arrived in New York, it was a friendship that grew over time.

Rabbi Sherer was clean-shaven and wore modern suits, but he was as Orthodox as Rabbi Besser. Rabbi Sherer was also very much a part of the world around him. He knew major political leaders and cultivated their friendship. It was a perfect fit in personality and political views. The two rabbis became close friends.

"He was a marvelous speaker, a very strong speaker. Perhaps I admired this because I don't think I am. He also

worked not twenty-four hours a day but thirty-six. I don't
know how he did it. He would often call me late at night
and he was still working. He was very well organized and accomplished a great deal. I loved this man."

They traveled together—to conferences and political
meetings—and they were often seated together. Moses
Sherer became the head of Agudah in America; when it
made its annual visit to Washington, his charisma made the
event a magnet for important officials. Members of
congress, the Supreme Court, and the administrations from
Presidents Reagan to Clinton would always take time to
meet with them, not only because it was wise politically (Orthodox Jews constitute a growing voting base that tends to
vote in unison), but because of Rabbi Sherer. Politicians on
both sides of the aisle respected Rabbi Sherer. But it was
conservative Republicans along with the Christian Right
that formed a special bond with Agudah. They were impressed with the deep morality and strong religious convictions of its members. On certain lightning-rod political
issues—like abortion and school vouchers—there was much
agreement. Rabbi Besser loved these meetings in Washington where he could see, firsthand, how both sides of the
aisle came together around Rabbi Sherer.

In the 1980s, it was Rabbi Sherer who encouraged
Rabbi Besser to take a more active political role by becoming a member of the U.S. Historic Preservation Commission. The commission was set up by the State Department to
protect, among other things, cemeteries abroad. He has
been a member of the commission ever since the Reagan
administration, offering his time, along with his vast knowledge and his contacts in Eastern Europe.

On one of the many trips the rabbis took together, they

sat next to each other on the plane coming back from Europe in 1998. They talked far into the night about Agudah, politics, and the future of the Jewish people. It was on this trip that Rabbi Sherer confided to his friend that he wasn't well and probably shouldn't have made this trip, but he felt it was vital. He said that when he arrived he would have to go directly from the airport to the hospital.

He did, indeed, go straight to the hospital and passed away just a few days later, on May 17, 1998. Rabbi Besser delivered the main eulogy at his funeral. Tributes came in from around the world. But for Rabbi Besser, it was much more personal. It was the loss of his closest friend.

NINE

THE PARTNERSHIP

A business partnership is as delicate as a marriage. When it works, each partner complements and brings out the best in the other. They can accomplish much more together than alone. And like a really good marriage, a truly successful partnership is not as common as people would wish.

This is a story of one of those perfect partnerships that on paper, at least, sounds highly unlikely—an elderly Hasidic rabbi and an American billionaire who felt more at home at a White House reception than in a shul. That Ronald S. Lauder ever even met Haskel Besser, considering their very different worlds, is a wonder. Or perhaps it was bashert, willed by G-d. The events that brought them together began with a very reluctant but inevitable trip to Europe more than thirty years after the war.

The rabbi had been all over Europe since 1946, including Germany in 1952. But he had not gone back to Poland. It wasn't until 1977 that Rabbi Besser finally traveled back to his home for the first time since he left, on September 1, 1939, and the trip touched some deep emotions he had held in check all that time. The trip took him to Warsaw, Cracow, Radomsk, Lezaisk, and, finally, Katowice. None of it was easy.

"I was nervous, even afraid," the rabbi recalls, looking back on his return. "This was where I grew up, where my home was. I went to school in this country. I knew this country.

"It was like visiting earth after I am deceased. The sky was the same, the buildings, the street—all were the same. But everything else was not." The swirl of emotions caught him by surprise. "There were new people there, yet I saw the other people, but they were all gone. It wasn't real."

He wasn't alone in his discomfort. People on the street looked at him as if he were a ghost. Most Poles had probably not seen an Orthodox Jew with a long beard and black hat since the war. When he encountered some anti-Semitic sneers and verbal abuse in Katowice, it actually helped bring him back to reality. As unpleasant as it was, it was also a live connection to the past.

One of the most difficult moments came when he stood outside of his childhood home, the apartment at 3 Dyrekcyjna Street (the name of the street was now Korfanty, changed by the Communists to honor a nationalist leader of Silesia before World War I, who was, ironically, an anti-Communist). He didn't knock on the door of the apartment. He did not want to explain who he was to the people who now lived there. It would have been too difficult to go inside anyway, so he just stood there for a while and looked up at the windows. When he went past his old synagogue, it wasn't there at all, a street now ran through the place where it once stood.

"The Germans didn't just burn it down," reports the rabbi. "They blew it up with explosives just days after they arrived."

Nearby, there had been a mikva (ritual bath), which was still standing but had been turned into a city bathhouse. He walked past his school and the street where most of his relatives lived. One of the only places where he found some peace was in Kosciuszko Park, where his nurse brought him every day when he was a baby and where his family used to take their walks on Shabbos. There was a pleasant restaurant in the park near where the rabbi was sitting, and the owner, a pretty young woman, came out and invited him inside. She seemed to know that he could not eat the food, but she offered him a Coke and asked him to sign her guest book. This small, kind gesture went a long way in helping him find something positive in the visit.

But Rabbi Besser had not returned to Poland to stroll down memory lane. He was there on a mission. He wanted to find the grave of the Radomsker Rebbe. It was something he had felt compelled to do since the end of the war. But if the trip back home to Katowice was difficult, the visit to Warsaw's main Jewish cemetery was a shock.

Jews are commanded to return to the graves of their family members on the anniversaries of their deaths to recite prayers and honor and remember them. (Hasidim make the same yearly visits to the graves of great rebbes and scholars as well.) The gravestones are usually uniform in appearance and inscription, with the name and dates of birth and death chiseled in Hebrew. But for rebbes and community leaders, the graves are more elaborate—there are special mausoleums called ohels that look like small stone houses that set their graves apart.

Almost every ohel, along with many of the graves Rabbi

Besser saw in the Warsaw cemetery that day, had been destroyed. And even worse, most of the graves had actually been dug up. These obscene acts had not been committed during the war by Germans. It was the Poles who tore them apart *after* the war, looking for gold and silver they foolishly believed Jews buried along with their dead.

"It was scary. There were holes everywhere and you could even see human bones in the dirt. I told the other people who came with me to go on, I would search by myself. Truthfully, I really wanted to be left alone."

He felt a strong kinship with the people who were buried there. And so, in spite of the upsetting scene, a strange sense of peace came over him. Perhaps it was because he was physically close to his rebbe for the first time since 1939. Perhaps it was because here—not in front of his old apartment or his school in Katowice—he finally felt at home, surrounded by his people. Rabbi Besser spent the entire day in the cemetery looking for the rebbe's grave.

He wasn't searching blindly. He had a lead. After the war, he had met a man who survived the Warsaw Ghetto and the gas chambers, and kept a diary of the entire time. The diarist recorded that the Radomsker Rebbe died August 1, 1942, on a Shabbos. On that day, in what can only be described as a riot of death, Ukrainian SS troops went from house to house ordering Jews to come out on the street, where they mowed them down with machine guns. The rebbe must have known what was coming and he simply refused to come down. When his followers implored him to come down saying, "Please, they'll come up and kill you," his only answer was, "Then I'll be buried."

That, of course, is exactly what happened. The Ukrainians came up the staircase, knocked down the door, and shot him along with his wife, daughter, and son-in-law. And an

entire noble rabbinic dynasty came to an abrupt and shat-
tering end in a blood-spattered apartment.

With so many corpses accumulating on a daily basis,
the Jewish victims were buried in mass graves. But because
of who he was, Jewish volunteers had taken his body along
with those of his family to the nearby Jewish cemetery and
buried them. Although Jews were not allowed to leave the
ghetto, the Germans did allow the Jewish burial society (volunteers who perform this function in every Jewish community) to pass through the wall in order to remove bodies.
This was not done out of respect. The Germans did not
want epidemics to start, which could easily spread to their
soldiers.

The diary of that day said simply that the Radomsker
Rebbe was shot, how it happened, and that he had been
buried. But it also gave one crucial detail—it said that he was
buried near another Hasidic leader, the Novo Minsker
Rebbe, who had died a decade earlier. If he could find that
grave, he might be able to find the Radomsker Rebbe's grave.

Half archaeologist, half detective, the rabbi began with
a prearranged meeting with the cemetery's caretaker. It was
not a successful start.

"The first thing I noticed was that he was drunk and it
was only nine in the morning. He also came up to me with
an outstretched hand. Foreigners had come there before."

The caretaker took Rabbi Besser to what he claimed to
be the grave of the Novo Minsker Rebbe.

"I asked how he knew this was the right grave, since
there was no longer a marker."

"How do you think I know?" came the rather belliger-
ent response. "I have a piece of the matzeiva [tombstone]."

The rabbi thanked him for his trouble, gave him some
money, and stayed there, sifting through everything stone by

stone. He was there from seven in the morning until four in the afternoon when it began to get dark. By the end of the day, he found another piece of shattered stone with three Hebrew letters: Chet-Taf-Nun, which means "son-in-law." So this was not the grave of the Novo Minsker Rebbe but that of his son-in-law, the father of the famous American rabbi and scholar Abraham Joshua Heschel.

After he returned to the States, Rabbi Besser took this information to the present-day Novo Minsker Rebbe, who was also a leader in Agudah, and asked if he knew where his grandfather's grave might be located. The rebbe didn't know, but three years later he sent Rabbi Besser a picture of the grave taken before the war. In the picture there was another important piece of the puzzle—visible names on three nearby graves.

With this information, Rabbi Besser went back to Poland in 1983 and found the grave in the photo almost immediately. Right near it, there was a large stone with nothing on it. This, he deduced, must be the grave of the Radomsker Rebbe along with his family, who had all been murdered on that day in 1942. There was nothing else nearby that remotely resembled a gravestone, and it made sense that there would be no name. In the Jewish tradition, a gravestone is usually not set until the first anniversary of the death. The rabbi died in August and the Warsaw Ghetto was liquidated the following April. All surviving Jews were sent by train to Treblinka and either put in slave labor camps or gassed. There were no Jews left in Warsaw to take care of such details. Over the next decade, Rabbi Besser— with the help of others—rebuilt the site and had the names and dates of the rebbe and his family inscribed on the stone. Eventually, Rabbi Besser helped rebuild more than sixty ohalim (rabbinic tombs) in Warsaw.

The importance of finding the Radomsker Rebbe's grave was multileveled. It allowed Rabbi Besser to honor this great man who had such a profound impact on his family. It also gave him a chance to stand near the rebbe and feel a personal connection to a brilliant dynasty that was completely lost. It gave the entire Jewish world the opportunity to honor one of its outstanding tzadikim (righteous Hasidic rebbes). And now, almost forty years later, someone could recite kaddish over the grave.

Viewing the destruction on that first visit, the rabbi realized that there were no longer enough Jews in Poland to tend the Jewish cemeteries, and the Polish Communist government was not about to do it. On a visit to Jerusalem, Rabbi Besser raised this issue with the Gerer Rebbe, probably the most important Polish Hasidic rabbi to survive the war. The Gerer Rebbe encouraged him to find a way to solve the problem. He even gave Rabbi Besser a substantial contribution from his personal savings to help start the work.

Rabbi Besser then went to the Polish government and negotiated a special agreement: if Agudah were given control of all Jewish cemeteries, it would pay for the upkeep. The problem was not getting the Poles to agree to allow a Jewish organization to pay. No one was paying for upkeep anyway—there was no upkeep—so the government would not have quibbled with that part of the deal. The problem was getting the government to cede *any* control at all to a foreign organization, let alone a Jewish one. Predictably, however, the rabbi befriended even the most hard-nosed government officials, including Poland's minister of religion, and the deal was signed.

This story now goes back across the ocean to Brooklyn, the epicenter of one of the most vibrant postwar Hasidic movements—that of the Lubavitcher Rebbe, Rabbi

Menachem Schneerson—in Crown Heights. After the war, this man developed a huge following that numbered in the tens of thousands. All of them wanted to be near him and at specific times during the week, thousands of people lined up for this honor. It was this rebbe's particular custom to hand out dollar bills to each person who came to see him— a reminder of tzedaka, the commandment to give to charity. People were supposed to pass these dollars on to charity, but truth be told, many people gave away other dollars and saved the ones that came from the hand of the rebbe.

One day, Mrs. Besser went to Brooklyn and waited in line to talk to the rebbe. Mrs. Besser was, in fact, related to the rebbe, and she was always allowed to go right to the front, but skipping a line wasn't Mrs. Besser's style. When it was finally her turn to have a word with him, the rebbe noticed she was alone. He asked where her husband was. The term "bet hachaim" is the Hebrew word for cemetery, but it is a euphemistic one. The literal translation is "house of the living." It is believed that if a person is righteous, his or her memory will go on living even after death. Since the Talmud tries to put a positive spin on all things, it focuses on that premise. Mrs. Besser told Rabbi Schneerson that her husband was in Poland, working on the bet hachaim.

The Lubavitcher Rebbe, aware of Rabbi Besser's work, leaned toward her and said, "Tell your husband he should also remember the chaim (the living), not just the bet hachaim."

It was a play on words. But there was also a message. The Lubavitcher Rebbe was telling Rabbi Besser that although his work with Polish cemeteries was important, he should also focus his attention on Polish Jews who are still alive. When Mrs. Besser passed along the rebbe's comment, the message was clear to the rabbi. But he wondered, what could he do for the living Jews in Poland? Most of those who remained (an estimated five thousand) still hid their religion. Many didn't even know they were Jewish. Even if a Jew in Poland in the 1970s wanted to eat kosher food, it was impossible. There was none.

"They had a slaughterhouse, but there was no shochet [the man who slaughters animals in the kosher fashion]."

By 1985, Rabbi Besser was traveling to Poland at least once a month, to give lectures, to offer private council, to make inroads with the government. These were long, exhausting days. Besides the work during daylight hours, people would wait for him to ask him personal questions when he returned to his hotel. His presence there had spread by word of mouth and the rabbi realized that there might be more Jews in Poland than he first thought. He was answering a variety of questions and dealing with personal problems in the hotel lobby until four or five in the morning.

On his way back from one of these exhausting visits, the rabbi stopped in Vienna for a meeting of the international arm of Agudah. During this trip, all of the rabbis were scheduled to visit the American embassy at the invitation of the ambassador, who was Jewish. Although the visit had been set up long in advance, the ambassador had suddenly been called out of town and no one at the embassy knew exactly what to do with this group. The chargé d'affaires called an aide to the ambassador and said that a group of Orthodox rabbis was in the building. The meeting couldn't be rescheduled since the rabbis were only in Austria for a brief time. So the aide did what she could. She served soda, since it was the only thing she could find that was kosher.

But during this abbreviated visit, the aide spoke with the rabbi and Mrs. Besser, who had accompanied him on this particular trip. The subject of Poland came up and the aide asked what they had been doing there. When the Bessers explained their attempts to get kosher food into the country, the aide became more interested. It turned out that the ambassador had also been looking for a way to help the Jewish population in Eastern Europe. The aide thought the rabbi should meet the ambassador.

Ronald S. Lauder came from one of the wealthiest families in America. His mother is Estee Lauder, the founder of the multibillion-dollar cosmetics company that bears her name. He had already distinguished himself in business and politics. Now, he was serving as U.S. ambassador to Austria— appointed by President Reagan. When Ronald Lauder took that posting, no one knew that he would take the reins of the embassy during one of the most complicated moments between the two countries since the war.

Kurt Waldheim, the former UN secretary general, was back in his native Austria. He left his position as secretary-general at the United Nations in disgrace after it was made public that he had served in the SS during World War II. At first, Waldheim denied it. But more and more documentation, including pictures of Waldheim in uniform, came forward. Further information showed that Waldheim's unit, stationed in Greece, had been involved in atrocities in 1942.

The controversy brought out the worst in the Austrians. Instead of questioning whether this man did the right thing in lying about his past, the Austrians began to cast blame elsewhere. One common remark was that this entire problem was being blown out of proportion by outsiders, especially foreign papers like the *New York Times*, an old code word for Jews, since the paper has been owned by a Jewish family for over a hundred years. Almost fifty years after World War II, it seemed nothing had changed: Austrians were still blaming Jews for problems that they, in fact, created.

As if to tell the world what they thought of this whole unpleasant business, the Austrians didn't criticize Waldheim. They elected him president. It was only a ceremonial post, but the message was transparent.

Ronald Lauder thought of himself in several different ways. He was a proud American, he was a New Yorker, and he was an active Republican. He knew a great deal about business, art, and foreign and military affairs. But he never really thought of himself as Jewish.

"I was—at best—a three-day-a-year Jew," he admits. That means he went to synagogue on the High Holidays in September and a Seder at Passover. That was it. He certainly never went to shul on the Sabbath, lit candles on Friday nights, or understood most of the prayers.

"I had no background," says Lauder. "I really did not have any connection."

Ronald Lauder had always loved the city of Vienna. And like everything else that interests him, he studies it, learns it, and lives it. One day, he was walking down a street in the second district called Templegasse, and he saw something odd. In this city that takes its architecture very seriously, there in front of him stood a glaring incongruity—an ugly parking garage on a street of beautiful ornate buildings. The ambassador asked people on the street what was there before the garage was built, but no one seemed to know. Or no one wanted to admit that they knew. Finally, one passerby stopped, looked at him, and told him the truth.

"The most beautiful synagogue in all of Europe once stood there," the stranger told him. "It was burned to the ground on Kristallnacht."

Between the Waldheim affair and those passersby who refused to tell him the truth, something happened within

Ronald Lauder. For the first time in his life he had witnessed raw anti-Semitism. And it made him furious.

Around the same time, the ambassador and his wife, Jo Carole Lauder, met a young rabbi named Jacob Biederman, who had started a small school for the children of Russian immigrants. Vienna had become a way station for Jewish émigrés leaving the Soviet Union. A deal had been brokered in the 1970s between the Soviets, the United States (spearheaded by Senator Henry Jackson), and Israel to allow Jews to leave Russia. Since the Russians couldn't allow their Jewish emigrants to go directly to Israel for fear of angering their Arab political partners, they sent them instead to Vienna. What they did later was their own business. For its part, Austria was trying to improve its image, attempting to become a quasi-Switzerland in the international community.

"These new immigrants didn't speak German," Ronald Lauder says, recalling their predicament. "They didn't know the customs of Austria. And they didn't know anything about Judaism, since it was illegal to learn it in the Soviet Union. They were simply stuck in this strange place."

Although Lauder had little in common with these immigrants—he may as well have grown up on a different planet—the sight of those children had a profound impact on him.

"I kept thinking, there but for the grace of G-d, I could have been in their shoes," he remembers. "So I told Rabbi Biederman I would be very interested in helping, but I really didn't know what I could do."

Rabbi Biederman and his wife showed the Lauders the one-room school and the ambassador could not get the faces of those children out of his mind. Ronald Lauder bought the apartment next to the one used for the overcrowded school, to give it some breathing room. Then he bought the next apartment. Eventually he bought the entire building.

It was around the time of that first school visit that Ronald Lauder noticed something odd on his daily schedule, which his secretary prepared every morning. There was another rabbi coming in that morning.

"I had always been interested in Orthodox rabbis because they were so different from anything I knew. At the same time, I always felt they wanted nothing to do with me because I was such a nonobservant Jew.

"But when I met Rabbi Besser," remembers Lauder, "he smashed the image I had of an Orthodox rabbi."

The meeting had been set for ten o'clock and as the two men began talking, one from the Hasidic world, the other from the secular, an almost immediate bond was forged. Each heard the other's vision for the future of the Jewish communities of Europe. And each saw in the other, perhaps, an element of what had been missing in their own method of achieving those goals. Rabbi Besser had the knowledge and understanding of the problem: Lauder had the means and skill to carry out the solution. They talked so long and so intensely that they lost track of time.

"My secretary would interrupt us to keep me on my schedule and I kept canceling the other appointments I had that morning. Then I started pushing off my lunch meeting from noon, to twelve-thirty, to one, to one-thirty. I finally and reluctantly had to leave because I could not cancel it."

The two men agreed to meet again during the rabbi's next trip.

Ronald Lauder's worry that Rabbi Besser would discount him because he was nonreligious turned out to be unfounded. The rabbi saw something that drew him to this nonobservant ambassador from an elite background.

"I believe in nobility," says the rabbi. "Ronald is not a common man. He is a noble man. He has a natural grace. Not all wealthy men have these qualities—far from it. I have seen men of great wealth be very coarse. And at the same time I have seen very poor men who have this fine strength of character. For all he has done, for all he continues to do, I think Ronald is a noble person with a very kind heart."

It was during the second meeting, in a hotel in Vienna, that the two men went over the problems facing Jews in every Eastern European country, one by one. Even though the countries were quite different, the situation for Jews was the same: those who had not been slaughtered had been hiding since the 1930s because that's how they had learned to survive. Why would these people live openly as Jews when that option went against every survival instinct in them? There was state-sanctioned anti-Semitism that was used whenever it was in the interest of the Communist Party.

Ronald Lauder had been working on an idea that came directly from his Austrian experience. He was going to create a foundation that would focus on the problems facing the Jewish population of Eastern Europe. In his vision, a new generation of Jews would be born in the very place where Hitler tried to wipe them out. In his usual forthright manner, the ambassador looked at the rabbi and told him he wanted him to work out of the Lauder offices in New York. He wanted the rabbi to move in immediately and direct all of his efforts to this end.

"We've never written anything down," Lauder observes. "We've always done it on a handshake. And it's been a wonderful relationship. He's changed my life and he's changed the lives of countless Jewish children in Eastern Europe."

In 1987, when his posting at the embassy in Vienna was over, he returned to New York and created the Ronald S.

Lauder Foundation. He wanted to give Rabbi Besser a leading role in the foundation, but the rabbi demurred. They
settled on the title: chairman of Poland, meaning he was in
charge of all of the foundation's efforts in Poland. In truth,
his work encompassed all of the countries where the foundation worked.

"Rabbi Besser gave the Ronald Lauder Foundation in-
stant credibility and substance," observes Malcolm Honlein,
the executive director of the U.S. Conference of Presidents
and someone who knows both men. "Through his contacts
in Europe—both personal and institutional—he understands the language and knows the history."

On the surface, a Hasidic rabbi in the corporate corri-
dors of a midtown office building seemed like an odd arrangement. When the other staff members first saw this
elderly rabbi come into the office, they didn't know what to
make of him. But within a very brief time, the rabbi became
everyone's favorite, from the retired U.S. Army colonel who
served as chief of staff to the Irish-American secretary.

Almost immediately, Rabbi Besser received one more
very important seal of approval. Shortly after he moved in,
Lauder introduced the rabbi to his mother, Estee. The rabbi
and Estee spoke privately for half an hour.

"She was very talkative," recalls the rabbi. "You could
see she was very sharp."

Afterward, Estee Lauder, one of America's greatest
business minds of the twentieth century and one not given
to emotional first impressions, gave her son her appraisal of
the rabbi. She confirmed her son's impression of the rabbi,
saying *this* was a man he could trust.

Another stamp of approval came from Marjorie Federbush, who eventually became the executive vice president of

the foundation. Federbush grew up in Hamilton, Ohio. After graduating from Wellesley College and coming to New York, she became a close friend of Ronald and his wife, Jo Carole. She and her husband, Alexander, were both Jewish, but Reform. For this reason, it seemed a bit odd when Lauder asked Federbush to accompany the Orthodox rabbi on a trip to Poland.

"I think it is to Rabbi Besser's credit," she observes, "that the trip was such a huge success. He went out of his way to include me and teach me so much of what he knew. I think it's an example of the unusual nature of the foundation, that an Orthodox rabbi and a Reform Jew like myself can work so well together, forging a friendship, and accomplishing a great deal."

Both the rabbi and the ambassador were realists from the outset. The old world that Rabbi Besser knew as a boy— a world with three and a half million Jews in Poland and one million Jews in Hungary—would never come back whole and intact. At the same time, their goal of sparking an interest in Judaism in the younger generation was not a modest one. Many people wondered aloud why these two men were even bothering. And more than a few Jews were outraged that any time or money at all was going to these countries which were the graveyards of millions and still infused with anti-Semitism.

"Teaching my generation is just not possible," notes Ronald Lauder, who was born during the war. "They were brought up under Communism. They had no connection to Judaism, nor did they know anything about it. But I was amazed to see that their children had an active interest. And I believed that through the children, we could create a very vibrant Jewish community. I was determined to build the best schools I could for these children."

Rabbi Besser acknowledges that although he understood their work was important, he still never expected to
witness the change that has occurred.

"Fifteen years ago, if a Polish Jew could hide himself,
he would hide," the rabbi admits. "But at the beginning of
the new century, the Jews of Poland suddenly and surpris-
ingly became proud of their Judaism.

"They learned what it means to be Jewish. They received some token Jewish education, which made them feel
worthy and important. Through the Lauder summer camps,
set up for both children and adults and staffed by educators
from Israel and America, they came in contact with Jews
from other countries. This gave them a sense that they were
part of a larger community.

"The collapse of Communism helped, but that's only
part of the picture. I started my work when Communism was
very much intact and I found an interest in Judaism even
then. Yes, the collapse made it easier, but the interest had
been sparked even before."

More than fifteen years after they began this work,
Lauder also sees the changes that have taken place.

"We see the generation between thirty-five and sixty
taking an interest. But things have been reversed. While
most people learn their religion from their parents or
grandparents, we see children coming home from school
and teaching their parents. Jewish stores are opening up.
After the war, there was a real fear of having a store with a
Jewish name in the front. Now we see those signs. Granted,
we will never re-create what was, but as long as you keep that
flame alive, two things are going to happen. One, you can
build a community, and two, Hitler will not have won."

From that first school started in Vienna, to new modern preschools, elementary and high schools throughout

Central and Eastern Europe, the foundation made its im-
print. But just as Rabbi Besser defers any credit to Lauder,
the former ambassador also defers credit for any achieve-
ments of the foundation that bears his name.

"A great part of its success came from Rabbi Besser's
work," Lauder observes. "He gave these people hope for the
future. He told them it was okay to raise their children to be
Jewish. And it was okay to pray and wish for better things for
their children.

"It helps that Rabbi Besser is related—either directly or
indirectly—to almost every person he's ever introduced me
to," jokes Lauder. "I know that, theoretically, we are all sons
of Abraham, but he takes it several steps beyond."

The two men have traveled tens of thousands of miles
together. They have met with presidents and prime ministers as well as penniless immigrants and schoolchildren.
They have accomplished great things, always with a sense of
joy and humor.

"We were visiting a burned-out synagogue in Breslau,"
Lauder remembers. "We arrived at two in the afternoon by
private plane and were supposed to leave at four. But we
were told by the tower that we couldn't leave because the
only English-speaking people on staff had left for the day
and we would have to wait until tomorrow morning. So, I
said, Who do we know who speaks Polish? And there was
Rabbi Besser. We put him in the copilot's seat with a headset
over his yarmulke and had him translate for the pilot."

"An updated version of G-d is my copilot," quips
Ronald Lauder.

There had to be laughs wherever they could find
them because so much of the work was heartbreaking.
One night in a large room in Warsaw that was filled with
Jews of all ages, Lauder asked the rabbi if he knew any

Yiddish lullabies. The rabbi sang one, then two, then three. By the second song, the older people first began mouthing the words, then some tentatively joined in. Finally, almost everyone was singing with tears streaming down their faces. The rabbi's singing had sparked distant memories of their mothers singing to them so many decades ago.

IN THE SHADOW OF THE HOLOCAUST

Everywhere they traveled, there were always people who came up to Rabbi Besser and asked to "have a word" with him. Once, when he was walking out of a cemetery, he was stopped by a woman who asked if she could just walk around him in order to see him from all sides.

"I wondered if this was some kind of hocus-pocus," he recalls.

The woman then explained that he reminded her of a grandfather she hadn't seen in over fifty years. In fact, she hadn't seen anyone who looked like him since the war.

Most often the people who came up to him had discovered they were Jewish late in life. Sometimes a mother on her deathbed confessed to her child that she was not the true mother and that, many years ago, a Jewish woman handed her a child on a gray day during the war in her last hope of saving it. Sometimes, people would sift through letters and documents after the death of a parent and find a name they had never seen before—only to discover that this person was their real parent. These children were raised as Catholics in a very Catholic country. Often, the news didn't come as a complete surprise. In inexplicable ways, they seemed to know they were different. In all cases, their motives for talking with Rabbi Besser were personal and complex. The rabbi became a spiritual adviser, a confidant, and even a marriage counselor. Most often the people who discovered they were Jewish were married to non-Jews, and this raised a new series of problems. The non-Jewish partner hadn't signed on for this eventuality—sickness and health, yes, but a Jewish spouse was another matter.

Once, after one of his lectures, a senior official in the government came up to him and asked him for seven tapes of the talk.

"Seven?" the rabbi replied. "Why so many?"

The man explained that he knew seven women—four were married to generals and three to cabinet officers—who were Jewish and would probably like to hear them.

"It was like the floodgates opened up," the rabbi remembers of those days. The stories were always different, but in many ways always the same.

One night in a hotel, a woman came to Rabbi Besser and wanted a word with him. The woman's mother had lived in Zloczow (near Lodz). By 1942, the Germans were going from city to city, town to town, rounding up and killing all the Jews. The Jews of Zloczow learned what was coming and tried to send all the children into hiding. There weren't many options and so the children were sent into the woods.

Ten days later the children came back to the town but everyone was gone—their parents, everyone, just gone. Three girls were walking together. Two of them were sisters and the eldest was twelve years old. They heard that the Germans were coming back so they thought it would be better to go to the next village where there were no Jews.

Two of the girls looked Jewish, but the third had blond hair and could pass as a gentile. They asked the fair-haired girl to buy three train tickets for another town, but the girl was afraid. So the other two went and were able to buy the tickets. But when they came back, the other girl was gone. The Germans had come and taken her away. The two sisters went to the train and were able to get on, but once inside, a group of teenage boys began to taunt them. The boys said they looked Jewish. They said there noses gave them away and asked to see their papers.

One of the sisters began to cry. A tall boy stood up and came over to them. He said he didn't like to see girls cry and told her to tell the truth and he wouldn't hurt them. They admitted they were Jewish. The boy asked where they were going and they told him they didn't know. The girls got out at the next stop and the boy did, too, and began to follow them. The girls started to cry again, even though he promised that he wouldn't hurt them.

The tall boy took them home and hid the two girls for the rest of the war. After the war finally ended and the Germans had been routed, there were no Jews left anywhere around them. The older girl was only fifteen. And it was then—after the war had ended—that the boy declared his love for her. There was no one left in her family. Her parents, along with all of her extended family, had been killed. For saving her life, she married him. The woman telling Rabbi Besser the story was their daughter. The family lived like gentiles. One day, years later, this woman was in school and a boy brought in a cracker she had never seen before. It was matzo.

"What is that?" she asked.

"Go ask your mother," the boy replied. Everyone else in the town seemed to know her secret but her.

It was never easy to hide one's Jewishness in Poland. But for this particular girl, the pervasive anti-Semitism had the opposite effect. Instead of running from it and hiding, she wanted to know more about Judaism. In an unusual move in those days, the mid-1960s, her mother sent her to Israel for a two-week visit. She returned to Poland, but the trip had changed her. She became more active in Jewish affairs and eventually helped start a Jewish school.

The story was not an unusual one, although the outcome was unique. Some of the adoptive parents kept their children's background a secret to protect them from a situation that would obviously complicate their lives. Some, perhaps, didn't want to compete with the real mother and father. And some were afraid that the children would denounce their Catholicism and revert to Judaism, thus denying them entry to heaven.

One particularly poignant story illustrates the long, difficult relationship between the Roman Catholic Church and the Jews. A middle-aged lawyer in New York came to Rabbi Besser seeking help finding a brother he'd never met. During the war, a Jewish woman was hiding in various homes with her husband and six-year-old son. In one of the homes, the owner got drunk one day when the woman was alone with her son and attacked her.

The woman ran out into the street with the boy and both were struck by an oncoming streetcar. The mother was not seriously hurt, but the boy was not so lucky. He was carried to a nearby hospital and there the doctors had to amputate his foot. They also made a discovery. After the boy's pants were removed, they realized he was Jewish. The people at the hospital refused to hide the boy—hiding Jews carried a death sentence. But a local convent took him in. For a while, the mother was able to bring small items to the convent for her son, but soon the war took a more serious turn and she was unable to visit.

When the war ended, the woman had survived. She went back to the convent but no one seemed to know where the boy who had lost his foot could be found. She searched everywhere but to no avail. The search went on for years. She gave birth to another son in the meantime (the man who told this story to Rabbi Besser), but she could never find her older boy.

The family left Poland for the United States, but she never gave up looking. For decades, the mother tried every avenue to find her son. She dealt with the Communist government, the Vatican, even the United Nations, but to no avail. Finally, with the fall of Communism, the mother, who was now over eighty, along with her younger son who was in his forties, traveled back to Poland. After a great deal of searching, they were able to locate a mother superior from that convent, now retired for many years, who admitted that she remembered the boy.

But all she would tell them is that he was alive, well, and happy. She said that if she told them where he was living, there was a chance he might become interested in his Jewish past again. If that happened, then when he died, he would not enter heaven. The mother enlisted Rabbi Besser in the struggle but the boy—now a grown man—could never be found.

"They probably didn't want to tell her where he was because the child is a bishop by now," the rabbi surmised.

It's a complex relationship. Yes, the Church saved the boy's life, but it also denied a mother the chance to be reunited with her child. The situation raised another interesting issue. Throughout Poland, there are priests with Jewish last names, yet they are as Catholic as can be. They were raised Catholic and have devoted their lives to the Church. If their background is Jewish, at this point it's almost irrelevant.

Rabbi Besser's work continued to spark criticism within his own community. "It is an accursed country," he was told. "It should just be ignored."

But for Rabbi Besser and Ronald Lauder, satisfaction came from watching young children light candles on Friday nights and say prayers. It came from watching young boys putting on tefillin in cities where people were convinced Jews would never walk the streets again. It came from seeing the pride in the faces of teenagers at a summer camp singing Hebrew songs and dancing traditional dances.

"When I first came back to Poland there were five thousand Jews left from three and a half million," Rabbi Besser recalls. But all of them were born before the war. The rabbi says he could not find one young practicing Jew in the entire country. "Not one. Today, although there still may be not more than five thousand Jews officially, there is one fundamental difference. Most of them are young and that is, essentially, thanks to one man—Ronald Lauder."

For Ronald Lauder, the credit goes to Rabbi Besser.

TEN

FAITH AND FAMILY

The study in Rabbi Besser's apartment is a large room. Bookshelves of dark wood surround two large windows that face 84th Street. In the spring and summer, the windows are usually open and, even though this is New York City, the most prominent sound is the wind blowing through the trees outside. There are over one thousand volumes on these shelves, most of them commentaries on the Talmud in Hebrew and Yiddish. Unlike some people who have large personal libraries, the rabbi has read all of his books not once but sometimes twice or more. Ask him a question and he will often get up and go directly to a volume on a shelf and find a passage that reinforces his point. He is less fortunate if he is looking for a stray piece of paper or a document on his large desk, which, like the desk in his office at work, is a scene of controlled chaos.

On one bookshelf sit the framed photos of many of the rebbes from those old dynasties. They are stern-looking men, with beards and side curls, and they are the men Rabbi Besser has admired from his childhood.

It is in this study that the rabbi sits and composes his commentaries, which he delivers at the shtibel on Shabbos and holidays. He says it takes him longer to find something to say these days, but he always manages to accomplish this feat, week after week, month after month, year after year. Shortly after September 11, 2001, the rabbi sat in his study trying to compose some thoughts for Rosh Hashanah that would both educate and comfort his listeners, who were still in a state of shock over what had happened to their city six days earlier. The rabbi lost a cousin on the airplane that crashed in Pennsylvania, and he searched the Bible for some thoughts that might make sense of the horror.

The smell of smoke was still wafting up the West Side. The newspapers and television were focused on this event. The entire nation was trying to comprehend the enormity of the catastrophe in New York, Washington, and Pennsylvania. In the midst of all this, it was the time for Jews to take stock of their lives and reflect during this very important and solemn holiday period.

The rabbi decided to look directly at the question that many people outside the Orthodox community (as well as some within it) were thinking: Where was G-d? Where is G-d when things like the World Trade Center, the terror bombings in Israel, and the Holocaust take place? In order to answer this, he thought about Abraham, one of the main characters in the parsha that is read on the first day of Rosh Hashanah.

"Abraham was the son of an idol maker. And it was Abraham who broke with his father's tradition, becoming the first human to believe in G-d.

"He looked at all of these tchotchkes (pieces of junk) and thought to himself: How can these silly little things that man makes determine the universe and every living thing in it?

"When people ask where is G-d in all these matters," he told the members of his shul, "they are really creating their own tchotchkes, just like Abraham's father. They want a G-d that will do what they want. It's really the highest form of self-centeredness. Who are these people to determine who G-d is and what He thinks?"

Terrible things happen in this world, things that make no sense: children get sick, stupid accidents take lives, there is injustice and intolerance, disease and hunger. There are many things Rabbi Besser does not understand. This doesn't mean, though, that he would ever question the motives of G-d.

"We are mortals. We will never, ever understand the workings of G-d, nor should we. At the same time, and this is important, we are not robots. We have a choice. We have a mind and our minds give us a choice to believe in G-d or not believe. If we did not have that choice, everyone would simply follow the rules and our faith would be meaningless. We can also believe in miracles and the great power of the rebbes, or not."

That choice—to believe or not to believe—is critical in trying to explain the logic and reasoning of someone like Rabbi Besser, who chooses the path of faith.

"I could question my belief in G-d but I don't. I find no reason to question it. I want to believe."

He finds it much easier with that belief, to traverse the problems that all human beings encounter and there is nothing timid about Rabbi Besser's belief. It permeates his heart and his soul. On this topic, he has no doubts: G-d created the world. The Bible is fact. We are all created by G-d. Pure and simple.

THE POWER OF REBBES AND MYSTICS

But Rabbi Besser knows it is not always so simple when it comes to miracles. He understands that the reason the Hasidic rebbes had hundreds of thousands of followers was because these men were believed to possess supernatural powers. That is also why Rabbi Besser is very quick to distinguish himself from the rebbes.

"I am a rabbi. I am not a rebbe. I don't possess the wisdom of these men and I don't have a following of tens of thousands."

By the classic definition, a rebbe is a Hasidic leader who has inherited his position from his father. He has spent a lifetime in preparation for this role and he has distinguished himself as a superior scholar. Rabbi Besser is a leader only because he was elected to be just that—a leader—but only of a small shul on Manhattan's West Side.

"I was elected only to interpret Jewish laws for my shul. And I am not a holy man."

Some happen to see it otherwise. Over the years, hundreds of people have brought prospective spouses for his approval. They have asked him to make special prayers for the sick, thinking, perhaps, that his prayers may hold greater weight than their own. Why people do this, why they attribute these powers to him, he does not know. He suggests it could be as simple as his appearance, with his long gray beard and fatherly looks. "Maybe it's just because I look like someone special to them."

He will certainly offer advice, but his advice is based on wisdom that comes from the study of Talmud and the experience of years. There is nothing magical or mystical about it. It is not beyond the realm of human experience. While Rabbi Besser is clearly a man with an innate intelligence that is most impressive, the rabbi is realistic concerning his abilities.

"There are no tricks here," he explains. "The mind is like any other muscle. You exercise it enough, it gets stronger."

But the Hasidic rebbes, from what he has witnessed, gather their abilities from some extraordinary place to which he does not have access. Hasidim believe these supernatural abilities come directly from G-d. Rabbi Besser thinks it may be because Hasidim want to believe and the strength of that belief creates the mysticism. But he has seen even skeptics change their minds.

Once, Rabbi Besser brought a nonreligious friend to see the Lubavitcher Rebbe, Menachem Schneerson. These audiences were almost impossible to arrange, but because of Rabbi Besser's close relationship with the rebbe, he was able to bring his friend to the rebbe's office late one night, the most highly prized time for a visit. That was when the rebbe stopped his daily duties and focused on his studies.

The man had a personal problem he wanted to discuss and when he went inside the rebbe's inner office, Rabbi Besser waited outside the door with some of the attendants. It turned out to be a long meeting. When it was over, the man came out looking somewhat dumbfounded. On the car ride back to Manhattan, he described what had happened in the rebbe's inner office, as the sun came up behind them.

Rabbi Besser's friend told him that before he mentioned his problem, the rebbe asked about his life, his family, and his profession. The man told him he was an engineer and the rebbe proceeded to discuss a new discovery that only those very active in the field of engineering would have known about. There had been some intricate and complex articles in trade journals, but none of it had

Rabbi and Mrs. Besser receiving dollars from the
Lubavitcher Rebbe, Menachem Schneerson *(right)*, in
Crown Heights, 1985. *(Family photograph)*

yet seeped into the mainstream press. But the rebbe spoke
about the discovery and its implications with the understanding of one of the greatest engineers in the world. His
friend was astounded. How—with all of the rebbe's obligations to his community, his religion, and the world—would
he have time to read such a specialized text?

That kind of expertise, according to Rabbi Besser, extended into many different fields, from medicine to world
affairs.

"He was not an ordinary human being. He seemed to
be able to read much more than the hours in the day permitted. I don't think he slept more than one hour every
night—once I saw him meet with people for three days
straight, only stopping to daven."

There are many other stories that back up these almost superhuman abilities of various rebbes that Rabbi Besser will not share because they involve the privacy of others. He will simply say that he has witnessed so much astounding insight throughout his life that he has no choice but to believe in their power.

For the skeptics and nonbelievers, these stories confound logic because they are based on belief, not science. And for generations brought up on the principle that scientific truth will always trump religion, these stories can easily be dismissed. Some will argue these rebbes simply demonstrate great wisdom and common sense and it would be hard to argue otherwise unless one is predisposed to believe in G-d and mysticism.

For Rabbi Besser, Rebbe Schneerson's understanding of engineering on its own may not have been divinely inspired, but he cannot discount the sum total of all he has seen.

He offers another example that can be taken one way by a believer and another way altogether by someone unwilling to believe. During the war, there was a large Jewish refugee community that fled Europe and wound up in Shanghai. After their arrival, the Japanese overran Shanghai. Now these Jews were no longer in the hands of the Chinese but under the control of Germany's main Axis ally. When the Germans pressed the Japanese to turn over the entire Jewish community, the Japanese military governor sent for its leaders. Fearing the worst, the community sent a small delegation including the Amshinover Rebbe, Shimon Kalish, along with someone who could translate through English (the one language they had in common with the Japanese).

The Japanese governor was curious. He did not understand why these Jews were singled out from all other

Europeans. When the Japanese general entered the room and sat down, he stared at the group for a long time—five or ten minutes—without saying a word. The atmosphere was very tense and it was obvious that the three Jewish men were nervous. Finally the governor broke his silence, speaking in Japanese with a quick, terse question, which was translated by one of his lieutenants into English. The English-Yiddish interpreter then translated it into Yiddish. "Farvoos hoben di Daitschen aich azoy feint—Why do the Germans hate you so much?" Without hesitation and knowing the fate of his community hung on his answer, Reb Kalish told the translator "Zugim weil mir senen orientalim—Tell him the Germans hate us because we are Oriental."

The Japanese governor, whose face had been stern throughout the confrontation, broke into a slight smile. In spite of the military alliance, he did not accede to the German demand and the Shanghai Jews were never handed over. When they were clear of the building, one of the other members of the delegation turned to Reb Kalish in gratitude and asked him how he came up with such a brilliant response so quickly. Reb Kalish gave him an odd, quizzical look and then answered with a question of his own.

"What did I say?" the rebbe asked. He had no recollection of the meeting.

Did he temporarily black out from fear or was his answer inspired by G-d? The rebbe clearly demonstrated quick thinking and his answer was certainly intelligent. But this is where the interpretation depends on the interpreter—believer or nonbeliever. Rabbi Besser believes Reb Kalish acted at that particular time and place as a conduit for G-d in order to save this community.

The rabbi knows numerous stories of women who had been unable to conceive a child and went to a rebbe for advice. One rebbe suggested specific prayers. Another rebbe suggested homemade medicines to be taken at very specific times. The suggestions varied and none of them fit the rules of modern medicine or science. But the advice was followed and the women became pregnant. Was it G-d's work? Was it belief in the rebbe? Was it the power of positive thinking, or simply coincidence?

In his own rabbinic way, Rabbi Besser answers these questions with another story.

Over a hundred years ago, there was a man named Yankel who was a follower of one of the most famous rebbes of Eastern Europe, the Rizhiner Rebbe (who was the grandfather of the Husiatiner Rebbe—the man who suggested Rabbi Besser marry Mrs. Besser). Yankel earned his living by running an arenda, a small hotel, which also had a bar. Every town in Eastern Europe had one and whoever had the contract for the arenda usually earned a nice living. Yankel rented this arenda from the nobleman who owned the entire town—a common occurrence in mid-nineteenth-century Eastern Europe.

But although this should have been a lucrative business, and people fought for these contracts, Yankel had fallen on hard times and was unable to pay his rent. When it came time to renew the lease, Yankel knew the nobleman would probably not grant him another one. But that was the least of his problems. He could be thrown in jail because he owed a year's rent. His wife suggested that he go to the Rizhiner Rebbe with a kvitol, a small piece of paper stating a problem and asking advice. But he was too depressed to even do that.

Yankel had a neighbor, Mr. Wolf, who was not well. He had serious ailments, which no doctor seemed to be able to cure. When Yankel's wife heard that Mrs. Wolf was going to seek advice from the rebbe, she asked if she could come along. The trip took three days. When they arrived and asked to see the rebbe, the gabai (the chief aid to the rebbe, like a sexton) explained that the rebbe would not see women. He suggested that they write the kvitol and he would take it personally to the rebbe.

They followed his instructions and the gabai disappeared. After a while, he returned with a response for each woman.

For Mrs. Wolf, who was seeking medical advice for her husband, the message from the rebbe was "Don't worry, everything was going to be all right."

Her face immediately brightened because those simple and positive words from the rebbe were enough to give her hope.

To Yankel's wife, the rebbe advised her husband to call a feltscher (a medical person who was not quite a doctor, but performed simple procedures). The feltscher was supposed to administer pijaukes (hot cups placed over small cuts). Mrs. Yankel explained that her husband needed to pay the rent. What kind of help would pijaukes bring? The gabai shrugged his shoulders. He didn't interpret the rebbe's suggestions; he simply repeated what the rebbe said.

Upon returning home, Mrs. Wolf told her husband everything was going to be okay and he believed it. Mrs. Yankel was too embarrassed to tell her husband the rebbe's advice. Wolf actually began to feel better. Yankel, on the other hand, tried unsuccessfully to secure a loan to pay back the nobleman. When the day of reckoning neared, his wife saw no alternative and told him what the rebbe had said. Now she insisted that he call the feltscher.

That same morning, a competitor went to the noble-man and began to needle him. He said, "Nu? Did Yankel give you the money?"

"No," said the nobleman, "but he is a man of honor."

The competitor persisted, poisoning the nobleman's mind, until finally he ordered two of his guards to go to Yankel immediately and bring him back in chains. When the guards arrived at Yankel's home, they found him on the floor bleeding from what looked like every pore in his body. They were frightened and left without asking any questions. They went directly to the nobleman and reported that Yankel had committed suicide. The nobleman was horrified and had his coach take him to Yankel's immediately. He found Yankel still on the floor—pale but still breathing.

"Yankel, you fool," he said. "You'd take your life over money? We've been friends for twenty-five years. Do you think I would throw you out? I forgive your debt," the no-bleman said, and ordered his guards to wash Yankel and give him something to eat.

The following week, the two couples—Yankel and Wolf—had a celebratory feast. Wolf was feeling better and Yankel's debt was not only forgiven, but he had a new con-tract. Later, they went to thank the rebbe. Yankel told the rebbe that when his wife relayed the instruction, he thought it was a case of mixed-up answers. He thought the rebbe had prescribed the feltscher for Wolf and that everything would be fine for himself.

When the Rizhiner Rebbe heard this, he told Yankel that he was indeed correct. He *had* prescribed the pijaukes for Wolf, but the gabai had mixed up the answers. But the rebbe also explained how things worked out in their favor.

"I didn't perform the miracles," he told them. "You did it with your belief."

"If you have faith," says Rabbi Besser, "then that alone can perform the miracle. But ultimately, everything comes from G-d.

"If you have a case in a courtroom," the rabbi explains, "and you have a brilliant lawyer on your side, that lawyer can succeed because he is persuasive with the judge. In the same way, a rebbe can succeed because he has so much power that he can persuade G-d on your behalf.

"If people don't believe in G-d, there is no amount of material that will make them believe. But, look, there is a moon and planets and stars. They are all there in perfect order. A nonbeliever will say it is all based on science. But how did the moon and stars come into such an order? Who put them there? Was it all just an accident? Does that make sense? It's interesting that Einstein said that the more he learned about science, the more religious he became."

Sometimes, of course, there are limits to the power of rebbes and mystics. They are not always correct. Rabbi Besser remembers that one of the defining qualities of the shtibel he attended with his father in Katowice was that there were a great number of kibitzers in the group. "They were always making jokes. It never stopped."

Once, the Radomsker Rebbe traveled to Czechoslovakia to get the blessing of the Munkaczever Rebbe (it was customary for the Hasidic rebbes to seek advice and blessings from other rebbes).

The Radomsker Rebbe had one child, a daughter, and he was hoping for a grandchild. About thirty Radomsker Hasids accompanied the rebbe on this trip and brought kvitols of their own. Each one lined up to see the Munkaczever Rebbe. One man in the group explained that although he had been married for a long time, he had no children.

The rebbe looked at him and noticed he had no beard.

"Nu?" the rebbe said, looking at his clean chin. The man explained that it was difficult to be in business in Katowice with a beard.

The rebbe brushed his hand across the man's clean-shaven face and said, "If you grow a beard, you are going to have one."

The man was jubilant, and immediately upon his return he stopped shaving. But almost immediately, when the man came into the shul, the kibitzers began to needle him.

"Nu?" they asked. "Is there any news?"

"It's early," the man explained. "Give it some time."

After about ten weeks, the kibitzers asked the man what exactly it was that the rebbe said. Did he say the man would have a child?

"No," the man said, "the rebbe said that if I grew a beard I would have one."

"Of course," explained one of the jokers. "The rebbe said that if you grew a beard you will have one—what you will have is a beard!"

Soon after that, Naftali was at the Radomsker Rebbe's office when the man walked in clean-shaven. No one said anything, but it was clear that he had given up. After he left, the Radomsker Rebbe told Naftali: "Look how lucky the Munkaczever Rebbe is. He got himself into a problem by promising this man a child. Both he and his wife can never have children. I was wondering how the rebbe was going to get out of his promise."

The rebbe's suggestion of growing a beard probably would not have worked in this man's case. But it was his apparent impatience and lack of faith that was seen by the community (and perhaps himself) as the reason for the failure.

When Rabbi Besser was younger and heard these stories, he was not an absolute believer in the powers of the rebbes. But his doubts were overcome by strange occurrences that he can only describe as spooky stories.

Rabbi Besser knows a couple that needed help conceiving a child. The woman was forty-three and close to the age when it is no longer possible to conceive. They went to a rebbe who told the woman to take a certain medicine, but added two important directives: the woman would have to remain in bed for the entire nine months of the pregnancy and, under no circumstances should she see a doctor until it was actually time to deliver. This was a strange dictum, but the couple chose to follow it.

The rabbi knew about this story because the husband came to him with a question when his wife was in her fourth month of the pregnancy. He asked Rabbi Besser if the woman could fast over Yom Kippur or if she should eat on the Day of Atonement because her health was at risk. Rabbi Besser told the man that it was not his call—this was something a doctor should decide. The man broke the directive of the rebbe and asked a doctor to see his wife. After a checkup, the doctor told them that the woman was not really pregnant at all.

The wife was very upset, not least because it had been very hard for her to stay in bed for four months. But the husband was dubious and took his wife to another doctor, one of the top obstetricians in New York. The second doctor told them that the woman was indeed pregnant. But, sadly, the examination had destroyed the pregnancy and the woman was never able to conceive after that.

Rabbi Besser also had his doubts about mystics who weren't rebbes, but there were situations he encountered that caused him to at least wonder about their powers.

Thirty years ago, the rabbi's younger daughter, Debbie, was having a difficult time choosing the right chusin (husband). She is an unusually attractive and intelligent woman and she had agreed to one possible match, but it didn't work out and she broke off the engagement.

On a trip to Israel around that time, one of the rabbi's sisters-in-law persuaded him to visit a Sephardic rabbi, who was considered to be a holy man with unusual powers. She was aware of the problem and she was a strong believer in these mystics. Rabbi Besser was not so inclined, but perhaps in an effort to keep peace with his sister-in-law and because of his own curiosity, he agreed to come with her for a visit in a poor quarter of Jerusalem.

"He was very pious, but not someone who would impress you at first glance." The man's clothes were almost in tatters. "He didn't seem to have a nickel to his name."

One thing did impress Rabbi Besser: the man didn't ask for any money. Instead, all he asked for were the rabbi's name, his wife's name, and that of his daughter.

He then sat down with paper and pencil and began scribbling down numbers like a wild mathematician. The process is called gematria—each letter in the Hebrew alphabet has a corresponding number and there is an entire field that studies the numeric declension of different words and phrases along with their mathematic counterpart searching out codes and insight.

After a long period of feverish equations, the man looked up at Rabbi Besser and explained with certitude, exactly where the problem lay.

"When your wife was pregnant with this girl," he said to Rabbi Besser, "she considered having an abortion [an anathema in the Orthodox community]. That's what has created the problem." He continued. "It is unclear to me just what will happen, but I will say that there are two boys with the same name who are very much in the picture. One of them will make a good chusin."

Rabbi Besser thanked him for his time and left the house.

"It was absolute nonsense. We don't believe in abortion and we never contemplated such a thing—ever."

Rabbi Besser knew he was right from the start—he should have listened to himself and not wasted his time with such nonsense. But later that night, he recounted the story to Mrs. Besser, once again adding that he could have saved some time that afternoon if he had followed his instincts in the first place.

"Wait a minute," Mrs. Besser stopped him. "Don't you remember what happened?"

Mrs. Besser reminded him of an incident that occurred in Jerusalem eighteen years earlier. One day, without warning, Mrs. Besser fainted and was taken to the hospital. What she didn't know at the time was that she was pregnant. The doctors examined her and informed her of the pregnancy, but said they thought there was a problem and recommended that she have an abortion. Mrs. Besser immediately said no. The doctors were insistent, so she put them off by saying she needed some time to think about it. That same afternoon, there was an Arab attack in Jerusalem and the hospital quickly filled up with casualties. With the doctors and staff preoccupied, Mrs. Besser quietly left hospital and that was the end of the discussion of abortion.

There were, of course, no more problems. The baby was fine. The doctors at the hospital were clearly wrong. But there had been the suggestion of an abortion, though not by the Bessers. The mystic rabbi's prediction, which seemed like nonsense earlier in the day, was suddenly viewed in a new context.

"It made me wonder," observed Rabbi Besser.

It turned out that there were indeed two young men with the same name who soon appeared on the scene. Debbie married one of them. Years later, she and her husband have a warm and loving family with rather exceptional children.

There are more personal stories Rabbi Besser has encountered that don't necessarily fit into the neat rules of logic.

Among the buildings owned by Naftali in Berlin, one was in the eastern part of the city. Although Naftali owned it, the deed said it was shared with his brother. This brother had been a co-owner of the building, but was having economic problems before the war and came to Naftali for help. Naftali gave him the money and in payment the brother handed over his half interest in the building. The brothers signed a note but never reregistered the change because of the political climate in Nazi Germany.

Although the rabbi knew about this arrangement, it never really mattered because the building was in the east and it was considered worthless. This, of course, changed with the dramatic collapse of Communism. Suddenly, the building became quite valuable. When the rabbi went to reclaim it, he was told that the deed was shared with the uncle's family. He knew this would happen and he also knew the truth—that the building wasn't really shared at all. He went to his cousin and told him the whole story. The cousin told him he would have to go to Berlin to see for himself.

Afterward, his cousin told him that although he believed him, there was no documentation and that it was probably better to proceed with the deed as written. Always a peacemaker, this would have been all right with the rabbi, but the rabbi did not own his half of the building either. He had a brother and a sister, and although both of them had passed away, he shared it with their heirs, and some of them were upset that Naftali's brother's family was insisting on a half share that really didn't belong to them. This is exactly the type of situation that can create a family rift.

Around that time, the rabbi was in Israel for the annual yahrtzeit (anniversary) of his parents' deaths. When he went to the cemetery to pray, he decided to walk over to his uncle's grave as well. While he was standing over the grave, he literally spoke to his dead uncle saying: "Uncle, you know the truth, I know the truth, but you have to see that your son knows the truth." Rabbi Besser doesn't normally do anything like this, but he remembered a story his father-in-law told him many years before. Beryl Ludmir had done the same thing and actually achieved results. Perhaps it was desperation to solve a family problem. In any event, he left for home shortly thereafter, but there was no sign forthcoming.

Weeks later, right before Passover, Mrs. Besser persuaded the rabbi to clean up his study in order to make room for family members who were about to arrive for the holiday. The rabbi gathered up several boxes of papers and brought them across the street to store in the basement of the shul. This was not the first time he had done that since there were already boxes of papers from previous cleanings gathering dust in the basement.

As the rabbi was leaving, he walked past one box and, for no particular reason, opened it up to see what was inside. On the very top was a paper that was dated 1972. It was signed by his uncle along with a notary, stating that he relinquished all claims to the building in the eastern part of Berlin. There it was in black and white. The matter ended, alleviating any strife in the family.

The rabbi understands skepticism toward mysticism. He understands it would be very difficult for someone who hasn't had the experiences he has had to share his belief. In the end, if someone believes in mysticism or in miracles or in the power of the rebbes, then it doesn't matter if a miracle is real or not. As in the story of Yankel and Wolf, if a person believes it is so, in that person's reality it is thus. Rabbi Besser knows that many of his friends in the non-Hasidic world would never understand his interpretation of these stories.

When Rabbi Besser was a young boy, because of his father's close association with the Radomsker Rebbe, he was allowed to stand right behind the rebbe during many of the great celebrations. There were thousands of people in the room, all hungry just to be near this man, but it was Haskel who was pressed right up against the chair, next to the rebbe.

"It made me feel so proud. I remember when I was six years old. I was standing next to him in a hot, crowded room. And I remember breathing in his smell that came from his perspiration. I believe that being so close to this man and breathing this in has kept me from committing sins throughout my life. I really believe this."

Rabbi Besser certainly understands the complexities of the world and of human beings. And still, he believes he has been kept from sins because he stood close to a holy man and inhaled the air around him when he was a small boy.

LIVING IN THE WORLD

Rabbi Besser has spent his life believing in G-d, avoiding sin, living by the principles given by G-d to Moses on Mount Sinai. He prays at least three times a day and puts on tefillin

Rabbi Besser at the White House Hanukah celebration,
December 1990 with Mrs. Bush, President George Bush,
Vice President Dan Quayle, and Mrs. Quayle.
(White House photograph)

every morning. He considers it his obligation to study the
Torah as much as possible. In short, he has lived an exem-
plary religious life, but not just because it was commanded.
He lives this way because he has found that it is easier and
because he enjoys it.

Given these strong principles, it could be difficult to be
surrounded by the secular world of New York City, but for
Rabbi Besser, it isn't difficult at all. The rabbi is very involved in the modern world—keeping up with almost every
item of news both international and local—but he also has
the ability to filter what he sees around him.

In the early 1990s, a perfume advertising campaign had
an almost completely nude photo of a reclining model

across every city bus in New York. When asked if he was offended by this intrusion, he remarked in all honesty that he hadn't seen it, even though he is out and about all day long. He pays great attention to the world around him, but when that world offers up something he finds offensive, he chooses not to see it.

The rabbi's strict moral code accepts as fact that there are devils that tempt humans and sins that can and should be avoided. He sees this, once again, as a choice that human beings have. But he is not judgmental and will never comment on or denigrate someone who does not live by this code.

Recently, though, he has begun to worry about his adoptive country. He worries about what he cannot avoid seeing around him: from the abusive language and actions of teenagers on the subways, to the conduct of high public officials, to the powerful hold that popular culture has on young people. He used to love Hollywood movies in the era of Spencer Tracy and Gary Cooper, but he is convinced that Hollywood has not produced a decent film in forty years. Although he still loves classical music, he finds popular music worse than noise. He sees in popular culture a degradation of morality that could eventually hurt the United States more than enemies from abroad.

At eighty, he remains a world-class multitasker. By the time he heads out the door at 6:30 every morning, he's already spent the past two hours preparing for his daily Talmud class and taking a glance at the day's headlines. He reads the entire *New York Times* and several Jewish newspapers later during breakfast. He keeps a schedule that most twenty-year-olds would find taxing.

One evening after he officiated at a wedding in a large hotel ballroom, he found himself in that time, after the ceremony but before dinner begins, when people are just standing around and talking. Instead of greeting the other guests, he sat down in a corner and began an informal Talmud class. Almost immediately he was surrounded by thirty eager pupils.

"Better to learn for twenty minutes," he advises, "than to gossip."

Whether he is on a bus or in a doctor's waiting room or just sitting in his office when the phone finally stops ringing, if there is no immediate work to be done, he pulls out the small copy of the Talmud he always carries in his pocket and studies.

On January 20, 1989, he was invited to the inauguration of President George H. W. Bush. Arriving at his seat ahead of schedule, he started reading the pocket edition before the festivities began. Meanwhile, two cardinals sat down on the chairs next to him.

"I see our friend is reading the Talmud," one cardinal said to the other.

After the rabbi confirmed the observation, one of the cardinals said: "I've heard the Talmud deals with every aspect of the human experience. Tell me, though, is there anything in it that relates to the inauguration?"

Rebbi Besser thought for a moment and told him there was indeed.

"You see," said Rabbi Besser, "you celebrate one new year holiday, but in the Jewish calendar we have several new beginnings. We have Rosh Hashanah, the beginning of our new year. We also have the holiday that happens to begin tonight, Tu b'Shvat, the new year for trees, and that includes Bushes, too."

FAMILY

Rabbi Besser loves his new country and believes G-d has been good to America because America has been so generous to the entire world. But there are certain tendencies he has seen—beyond the issues of morality—that he disagrees with strongly.

"When I came to America, I knew that things were different and I didn't want to be closed in my views, so I watched to see if there was merit to these differences. But I didn't like it when I heard children call their parents by their first names. I didn't like the movement of parents trying to make children their friends. Children and parents are not friends or pals. A parent is something different."

His feelings about his family are clear—he loves them all dearly—but he is not demonstrative. He does not hug or kiss his children or his wife or anyone in public. Part of this is because of his natural reserve; the other part is that Hasidic men and women never offer public displays of affection. Yet the love he has for his family is obvious to anyone around him. And the reverence in which his children and grandchildren hold him is powerfully clear as well.

Considering how even active, loving parents sometimes have serious problems with their children, the rabbi's children and grandchildren are unusual. His family has never had the problems that many contemporary families have, but he takes no credit for this, only stating, "I am lucky."

But he offers a story that may help explain his good fortune. A friend of his, an important Orthodox rabbi, was on a flight to Israel and one of his sons had dropped him off at the airport. There was a leading government official on the plane, and near the end of the flight, he came over to the rabbi and told him that he was not religious, but he had noticed the respect the rabbi received from his son at the airport, and the man wondered why he never had that respect from his own son.

The rabbi answered the question in a strange way. He said that religious Jews don't believe in the theory of evolution. The official gave him an odd look. The rabbi explained that he understood this was very hard to comprehend in the modern, scientific world. But, he said, if you believe that you are descended from monkeys, you will not respect the past.

"My son respects me," the rabbi told the man, "because I am one generation closer to Moses."

Rabbi Besser never played baseball with his two sons. He never showered affection on his two daughters. Yet the love they have for one another is real and strong. His older son, Shlomo, has difficulty at times speaking in public about his father because he holds him in such awe. His grandchildren adore him, even though he never sits down on the floor and plays with them. In some ways, he may appear austere, leading the congregation and even in his own home— but to see the smiles on the faces of his grandchildren and great-grandchildren when they see him—he is anything but austere to them.

On Shabbos and holidays, he sits at the head of the table—Mrs. Besser sits at the opposite end—and he looks very much like the family patriarch that he has become. He conducts the conversation and steers the topics, often with strong opinions coming from Mrs. Besser's end of the table, not always in agreement. There are few people who are able to hold their own with the rabbi, and Mrs. Besser is one of them.

One afternoon, sitting in his office with a visitor, the telephone rang. He picked it up and the conversation went like this:

"Hello . . . Yes . . . Yes . . . Yes . . . Thank you . . . Good-bye."

Following the call, a smile came across his face. The curious visitor asked, Why the smile?

The rabbi looked at his guest and answered: "Without question, the smartest thing I ever did in my life was marry my wife."

Mrs. Besser had simply called to remind him to take his medicine.

The rabbi has guided his congregation through difficult times. He has worked with heads of state on important matters that impact the Jewish community. He has changed the lives of more people around him in positive ways than this book could ever enumerate. He has brought honor to his G-d and his people. He is deeply thankful that he was trained well by his parents and teachers to believe in G-d and his rebbe. But, to his mind, the smartest and perhaps luckiest thing he ever did was marry his wife.

EPILOGUE

The rabbi has seen something happen within his lifetime that may help to explain Hasidism's astounding rebirth, after it was almost destroyed in World War II. Today, Hasidism is one of the fastest-growing segments of Judasim. That fact seems miraculous given that bleak night in Brooklyn shortly after the war when Rabbi Besser saw a shell of what the Hasidic community once was. In those dark days, he hoped to see a resurgence, but even as he prayed for it, he didn't really know how, or if, it would ever come about.

He now sees young boys and men wearing yarmulkes all around him, in contrast to the 1950s, when a leader in Jewish education in New York advised boys not to wear yarmulkes when they left the school grounds. Orthodox families are now present on America's Main Streets—from Disneyworld to Wrigley Field. And Orthodox shuls and schools are springing up in unlikely places like Des Moines and Albuquerque. But the reason for this rebirth, he thinks, is not all positive.

"The twentieth century turned out to be a terrible disappointment for many Jews," Rabbi Besser explains. "For two hundred years, Jews had finally been accepted into the world. But the modern enlightenment proved to be the first great disappointment because so many Jews who bought into it saw the end result when Europeans turned on them in the 1930s. You don't even kill insects the way they killed Jewish children.

"The second disappointment came in Communism, which was supposed to end poverty in the world. It only created more poverty and more suffering before it finally collapsed.

"The third disappointment came after World War II. The Germans and their collaborators were embarrassed by what they had done and the rest of the world shared part of that embarrassment for not protesting the massive genocide earlier. But now sixty years later all of those feelings of embarrassment seem to be gone and some even doubt that it ever happened.

"And, finally, the fourth disappointment happened in Israel. Herzl and the early Zionists believed that if Jews had a nation of their own, that would be the solution to anti-Semitism. Sadly it was not.

"In some ways it is the loss of faith in human beings that drives people to G-d. Usually Hasidism prospers after big tzuris (trouble)."

This does not, you may notice, fit the positive nature of Hasidism that the Baal Shem Tov created within Judaism.

"The Baal Shem Tov didn't have such a happy life," the rabbi explains. "But the point is that we must always work at it. Yes, things may be terrible, the world may disappoint you, but things could be worse."

In the end, what differentiates Rabbi Besser from much of the rest of the world is not his appearance or the strict codes of his religious conviction or even the kosher food that he eats. It's not even his belief in G-d or in the miracles of the rebbes. It is the culture of Hasidism that makes his world distinctly different.

Where some cultures revere sports heroes or tycoons or actresses of great beauty, in Rabbi Besser's world the people who are placed above all others are those who have succeeded with their minds. If one is a brilliant scholar in the Talmud and Torah, then that person carries rank in his community. If one is descended from brilliant thinkers and teachers, then that person carries the lineage of royalty. And if the scholar also happens to be known as a kind, decent soul, then that person is revered above all others. It's not just scholarship—you should also be a *mensch.*

In his shul, there may be joking among the members, but there is also tremendous respect shown for one another. Within his family, there is great warmth and love. And even outside this tight-knit circle, people who know the rabbi treat him with a special kind of dignity not often seen in today's world. It's not just because of his age or his appearance; his good-natured way seems to bring out the best in others.

"I suppose I'm reaching the end of my life now. I find myself thinking, What were my goals? Did I achieve them?"

He is pleased that Daf Yomi, reading the Talmud a page a day, has caught on with a popularity he never imagined. "It's my baby," he says jokingly, but also with great pride.

His work protecting the Jewish cemeteries of Eastern Europe has now been passed down to his elder son, Shlomo, who is the head of a committee that is part of the International Claims Conference. He knows it will continue.

His monumental effort to rebuild Jewish life in Eastern Europe with Ronald Lauder shines through the happy faces of children he sees in elementary schools and summer camps—Jewish children who are proud of who they are, where they came from, and where they are going. The very idea of a young boy wearing a yarmulke with pride walking down a street in Poland or Germany or the former Soviet Union is a miracle of its own.

Throughout his life, he has tried to make sure that all people who meet him come away with a positive experience. His smile is real, although this has not always been easy.

At times when most people would not be able to contain their emotions, after hearing some of the heartbreaking stories he has encountered in his life, Rabbi Besser has never lost his composure. He has never flinched—whether telling about a father losing all of his children or even about the loss of his own father and mother, brother and sister.

One late afternoon in the 1980s, at the start of the holiday of Purim, the phone rang and Mrs. Besser picked it up. A short while later, she came into the rabbi's study where he was preparing his talk for the shul. She mentioned to him that the weather looked very bad outside. He looked up and agreed. She said there were probably a lot of accidents on the highways because of the bad weather. The rabbi knows Mrs. Besser well enough to understand she wouldn't come into his study and give him a weather report without a reason. Mrs. Besser then suggested that perhaps he should take some time to bench (say the blessings). He understood this, too, because if someone is officially in mourning, he cannot bench. The rabbi looked at his wife and without asking what she meant, said that maybe he would bench now. She said she thought that would be a good idea.

When he completed this, she quietly told him that his brother had been killed in an auto accident as he was heading back to New York for the holiday. The Bessers had many guests in the house for the holiday, including his friends Ronald Lauder and Mrs. Lauder. Throughout the evening, he never mentioned it to anyone, not wanting to upset their holiday. More than his personal composure, the story demonstrates that even when tragedy interrupts the routine of the day, the commands of his faith come first.

The rabbi's mother and his sister, Rosa, had passed away earlier from natural causes. The loss of his brother, Akiva, left the rabbi the only surviving member of his immediate family. There were, of course, so many uncles, aunts, cousins, grandparents, teachers, and friends who all perished in the Holocaust. His rebbe and the entire Radomsker dynasty have been gone for over fifty years. When asked how he manages to hold his emotions in check when he talks about these things, he explains that it comes from training.

"You have to learn how to do it because of your position," he explains. "A rabbi can't let himself show those feelings."

He has succeeded at this admirably, but in his later years, some chinks began to show in that sturdy armor. At the weddings of two of his grandchildren, with whom he has always been particularly close, he showed a side of himself that few have ever seen.

There are seven blessings in a Jewish wedding service and in order to share the honors they are often chanted by seven different rabbis. The first blessing, being the highest honor, was of course given to Rabbi Besser at both weddings.

In each case, he fought back tears as he prayed. The family members and close friends who know the rabbi well understood just how unusual this was. For them, it only lent more importance and dignity to these blessed events.

Rabbi Besser's secretary, Basia, shares with him a passion for music and has a collection of CDs that would rival that of a classical radio station. One cold afternoon in March, she excitedly dropped off a recording of Beethoven's Ninth Symphony, knowing it is one of his favorites, conducted by Toscanini at Carnegie Hall in 1952. As was his habit, the rabbi began conducting with his arm as he sat and listened.

After several minutes the recording came to one of the rabbi's favorite parts.

"This is a coda I particularly love," he told a close friend sitting in his office.

Then he began to cry.

"First he cried, then I cried, then we both cried," the friend recalls.

"What a gift from G-d to be able to hear music," said Rabbi Besser.

"There is so much pain in this music," he went on. "Beethoven was practically deaf. He was in the decline of his life and yet he could still create this."

Part of what comes along with a long life is a flood of memories that is at times unstoppable. At these times all the heartbreak that has always been just under the surface is woven together with all the thankfulness for a joyous life, like a beautiful and complex symphony.

It helps remind us of the most miraculous gift of all from G-d, the gift of life.